Building an
Exceptional
Workplace
Environment

Building an Exceptional Workplace Environment

FAST52

LYNDA FORD

 Rome, New York

Published by Ardan Press
P.O. Box 110
Rome, N.Y. 13442-0110

Publisher's Cataloging-in-Publication Data
Ford, Lynda
    FAST52: building an exceptional workplace environment / Lynda Ford: Rome, N.Y.: Ardan Press, 2002.

        p.   ;   cm.
    ISBN 0-9723037-0-7

    1. Employee retention. 2. Personnel management. 3. Work environment. 4. Job satisfaction. 5. Industrial relations. 6. Management. I. Title. II. Title: Building an exceptional workplace environment. III. Title: FAST 52.

HF5549.5.R58 F67 2002   2002110392
658.31--dc2l   FAST 520209

06 05 04 03 02 •   5 4 3 2 1

Project coordination by Jenkins Group, Inc. • www.bookpublishing.com

Printed in the United States of America

Contents

Acknowledgments

Working on a book is an exhilarating as well as an intimidating process. This was especially the case in writing about a subject that has many intricacies and complexities, and bringing it to a level that is pragmatic and understandable with useable strategies. I'd like to first thank my clients, who have taught me much over the years, and provided valuable opportunities to apply many of the FAST52 concepts. Each has contributed to my professional growth, and in turn have grown and improved their own workplace environments.

Thanks to the staff at The Jenkins Group, especially Mareesa Orth and Nikki Stahl, for their guidance, expertise and professionalism . . . and somewhat more than gentle nudges in completing this book.

My colleagues have provided invaluable insight and expertise. Special thanks go to Michael Fain, Michelle Lee and Milly Valverde for their practical and clear-sighted comments. And thanks to Linda Madore, for her resource research.

My thank you list would not be complete without acknowledging two mentors and colleagues. I thank Alan Weiss for giving me sound, to-the-point advice and the guided push I needed (so long ago) in deciding to write this book. Bob Simmen has been an invaluable friend, guide and sounding board, and has been responsible for leading me to the best possible professional decisions.

And last, but certainly not least, is my family, who are always there to support and encourage me. My husband

Greeley Ford, sons Aaron and Daniel Ford and mother Helen Myers have provided me with much support, information and context. And where would I be without my sisters, Leslie and Bobbie. I thank you from the bottom of my heart for being a part of my life.

Introduction

The idea of FAST52 originated from countless discussions with managers and employees that revolved around the issue of employee retention. The most common comments were: "We need ideas that we can immediately put to use. We don't have time to do lots of reading, or attend seminars. We need something that can get us started toward improving the work environment. We need ideas that we can implement on our own."

The strategies in FAST52—Building An Exceptional Workplace Environment have been developed based on my own experiences with a variety of organizations. They have not been scientifically tested. They have, however, been used successfully in diverse work settings.

The FAST52 concept is based on the notion that if you can consider just "one idea a week" and put many of those 52 ideas to use, you'll see improvements. And, if you have access to just one idea each week, at the end of one year (52 weeks) you'll have laid a solid foundation for an exceptional workplace environment.

FAST52 is an acronym that stands for:

✦ Focused—Each FAST52 strategy is focused at the issue at hand. It is narrowly defined so that you are able to significantly impact the area that you've chosen.

✦ Action-Oriented—The FAST52 strategy is based on gathering momentum by taking visible actions. There is no room for lip service in FAST52 management; it is all about taking actions so that employees can see you building a better work environment. These are ideas that almost entirely within the manager's span of control. For the most part, there is no need to wait for higher levels of approval before implementation.

✦ Steeped in Simplicity—Each idea is based on a simple, easy to understand premise and is relatively easy to start and maintain.

✦ Timely—The ideas are timely; that is, they can be used immediately. This allows you to make just-in-time improvements.

✦ 52 Weeks a Year—Fifty two ideas, fifty two weeks. There's an idea for every week of the year.

The FAST52 concept allows each strategy to stand alone. So, if FAST4 makes more sense for you to start with than FAST1, that's okay. You don't have to go in order, unless that's your preference. FAST2 is not predicated on successfully completing FAST1; so jump to the middle or end of the book, if that's your style.

If you can use all of these strategies, that's great. But chances are you may be using some of them, or you may not be comfortable with others. Pick and choose what works for your organization. If you can implement on a long-term basis even a few of the ideas, you'll realize long-term improvement.

The Retention Connection

Information gathered from exit interviews conducted by our company last year indicate that employees leave for what we describe as controllable reasons. Controllable reasons are defined as situations that are directly within the company's control to take action and change. These include areas such as work environment, pay and benefits, relationships with supervisors and co-workers, scheduling, opportunities for advancement, opportunities for training and professional development, ethical issues, job fit and job duties. Uncontrollable reasons include areas such as relocation of a family member, health reasons—either the employee's or a family member, return to school, transportation issues, and general personal reasons. In all cases, more than half of the employees left due to controllable reasons.

This points to a company having control over more than half of the turnover problem. In all cases, work environment accounted for the most frequently cited reason why people left the company. Generally, departing employees felt that their opinions and contributions weren't valued and their relationship with co-workers, and especially supervisors, weren't satisfactory. It's no secret that the supervisor or manager is key in setting the tone for a satisfactory work environment.

Turnover costs have been estimated at anywhere from 50% to 200% of an employee's salary. If that number has you skeptical, then use a very conservative $3,000–$4,000 per employee. The following chart will help you come to that figure:

AREA	COST
Advertising Costs	
Pre-screening/Pre-interview Costs: Reviewing resumes and applications, preparing for interviews, fielding telephone calls, administrative paperwork, credential and other background checks	
Interview/Hire Costs: Conducting Interviews (1st and 2nd round), reference and other checks, physicals and other exams and screenings, telephone and administrative time, evaluating each candidate, making the offer (include negotiation time)	
Orientation and Training Costs: Include full orientation period and on-the-job training; learning curve time (not fully productive)	
Overtime/Contractor Costs: Other people that must cover the open position	
Other Costs	
Total	

Let's say your company has 300 employees, and your turnover is 20%. That equals 60 employees. Take that number times $4,000, and your turnover just cost you $240,000. That's almost a quarter million dollars. Even if just 50% of that is due to controllable reasons, you would save $120,000 in that year. That's substantial, and a very conservative estimate.

Loyalty Today

Gone are the days when people received a gold watch for the retiring after 25 years with a company. There is little stability, from both the employee and employer perspective. Long-term has a very different connotation today than it did even a decade ago. When a company does strategic planning, it often means a three-year or perhaps as much as a five-year plan. Ten year strategic plans are becoming a scarce commodity.

In light of the massive layoff's of 2001, employees are wary about becoming too comfortable with any employer. An employee's perspective turns to gaining as much as possible in the short-term, because there may not be a long-term career option with the employer. This causes employees to job-hop, and continually be on the lookout for the next best opportunity. Ten years ago, a resume with four jobs in five years would barely be looked at. Today, it's accepted as commonplace. If we asked employees if they'd like the stability of one employer, given fair pay and benefits and a decent working environment, most would probably say yes. However, this is not their reality.

Employers have turned to layoffs as a short-term strategy for cost cutting, and increasing shareholder value. We call it downsizing, rightsizing, re-engineering and optimum staffing. It is touted as an economic reality, and for these companies, cutting payroll is a matter of survival. Or is it?

What we've lost in all of this is the mutual loyalty between employer and employee. Each side views each other as a commodity; that is, as an object that helps accomplish the task at hand. Somehow the humanness in the employment relationship has been lost, or at least derailed. What the strategies in this book try to do is re-establish the human relationship. It relies on a mutual connection, and with that connection build a relationship that is steeped in trust. With that trust comes loyalty.

When we move to a position of mutual trust and loyalty, we find the very qualities that are needed for higher performance levels are right in our workforce. Creativity, innovation, risk taking, problem solving, decision making, leadership and open communication channels are just some of those qualities. They're right under our collective nose. Our employees have those qualities; they just may not have the right environment to showcase them. As a FAST52 manger, you'll be able to set that environment on a daily basis.

Ten Tips for Becoming a FAST52 Manager

1. Each person is an individual; there is no "one size fits all."
2. Use active listening skills. Frequently check for understanding.
3. There may be resistance when you start using some of these strategies. That's natural, and people may be distrustful at first. Encourage open and honest communication.
4. Set the tone for learning and improvement. Guide your employees and let them act as guides for each other.
5. It may sound old or trite, but always walk the talk. Make sure your actions are consistent with your values and beliefs.

6. If something obviously isn't working, then don't prolong the experience. Go on to something else.
7. Some strategies take longer than others to implement and to see visible results. Think about first implementing strategies that will give allow for immediate success. You'll be able to build momentum with your group.
8. You'll probably make at least one or two mistakes. Readily admit your shortcomings, and show that you're trying to make things right.
9. A facilitator or trusted colleague may be able to assist you in strategy implementation, or offer an outsider's view to help remove roadblocks from the path you're traveling.
10. You know your employees, the work environment and organization policy and procedures. So tweak the strategies as needed, and use your judgement in deciding how to introduce your group to each strategy.

And now, let the FAST52 journey begin.

FAST 1

Address Potentially Sticky Situations Head On

A RECENT HEADLINE IN THE LOCAL PAPER read: *"City codes officer suspended for insubordination."* It seems that the codes officer alleged to the newspaper that certain landlords receive preferential treatment from the codes department. When his boss asked him to sit down and explain the problem, the codes officer walked out of the room, precipitating the suspension. The codes officer claimed that the supervisor was well aware of his feelings. Needless to say, that supervisor is probably wishing she had addressed this issue before it hit the newspapers.

Small issue, smaller investment of time rectifying it. Big issue, bigger investment of time rectifying it. It's all about being proactive.

Most of us know that the earlier a sticky situation is addressed, the easier it is to fix. Here are a few tips on how to address potentially sticky situations:

✦ If it's in your department, go straight to the source. Don't talk to people who aren't directly involved. Talk to the person(s) involved.

+ Question them in a non-threatening way, using "I" messages to find out what's going on. Use open-ended questions. Rather than asking, "Is anything wrong?" say, "I sense that something isn't quite right. Let's talk about what might be on your mind." Come to an agreement about how to proceed.

+ If it's a department-wide problem, get everyone's input. If people are reticent about speaking out, arrange for private meetings.

+ If people are reluctant to speak in a group, use some type of checksheet that allows you to gauge the group's mood.

+ If it's outside your department, go to one of your peers (another manager) in the other department. Approach it from the perspective of fixing the *problem*, not the person or people involved. Use a collaborative approach.

Try this formula when there is a potential for conflict or misunderstanding based on a difference of opinion:

+ When I saw (or heard) _____

+ It made me feel _____

+ For these reasons _____

+ And now I'd like _____

+ In order to _____

Using some variation of this formula helps to keep emotions in check without escalating the situation.

FAST2

Allow Employees To Stretch

REACH FOR THE STARS AND YOU MAY AT LEAST touch the moon. How many of your employees are reaching for the stars . . . or anything? How many are stretching beyond what they think they're capable of accomplishing? To allow employees to stretch, a manager must first identify the competencies that are critical to organizational success, and then identify, in partnership with employees, opportunities to build on those competencies.

For example, if you've identified creativity as an important competency, what types of assignments can you offer employees that will allow them to stretch their creative spirit? Let's take a secretarial position. In what areas could that creativity be sparked? Some areas might be better forms, new ways of handling correspondence, more efficient use of the department calendar or more customer-focused methods of greeting people that come into your office.

Wherever that creativity is needed, here are a few guidelines to help make that stretch a productive one:

✦ Make sure both parties agree that the project is meaningful and will have impact on the operation.

✦ Provide guidelines to help the employee get started.

✦ Provide the necessary tools and support.

✦ Agree on the deliverable. In this example, the deliverable might be a better process for handling routine correspondence.

✦ Allow the employee some latitude in the means. In other words, unless the employee is straying far from the original intent (the deliverable described above), let them decide on the best way to get there.

✦ Use frequent checkpoints. It gives the employee opportunity talk about the project and lets you keep abreast of developments.

✦ Debrief. When the deliverable is complete, review the process. Talk about what went well and what needs improvement. Then, talk about the next "stretch."

✦ Positively reinforce and enthusiastically celebrate the successes. There's always at least one success!

At first you'll find that you must guide employees through the stretching process. But soon, something magical happens. You'll find that employees are taking the initiative to stretch . . . all by themselves! And isn't this what you're working so hard for . . . a self-motivated, high performance workforce?

FAST3

Ask for Your Employees' Recommendations on Job-Related Problems

D r. W. Edwards Deming, renowned quality expert, urged managers to *"find the problems. It's management's job to work continually on the system."* One of the best ways to find the problems and to work on them is to involve the individuals that are naturally a part of the process.

For example, if you're grappling with how to get better candidates to interview, talk to the people that are closest to the problem. This might include:

+ Employees that work in high-turnover departments. They'll be able to tell you what causes the turnover and what type of person it takes to work there.

+ Employees who work in low-turnover departments. They'll be able to tell you why their department has low turnover and what type of person best fits into that environment.

- ✦ Employees in your department. What makes them want to stay or go? What ideas do they have for getting good people through the door.
- ✦ People responsible for recruiting at your organization.
- ✦ Internal and external customers.
- ✦ Supervisors in other departments.
- ✦ If you're hiring recent college graduates, spend some time in their classrooms to find out what attracts them to an organization. If you're hiring high school graduates, visit the local high school. Teachers love it when business people come in to talk with their students.
- ✦ If you're hiring professionals, go where they go. Talk to them at professional group meetings and community and social events. Find out what attracts them to an organization. But beware: This isn't the time to recruit!
- ✦ Use focus groups at your organization to discuss specific issues.
- ✦ Use exit interview data to determine what's good and not very good about the organization, and then do something about it!

In a breakfast of bacon and eggs, the chicken is involved but the pig is committed! After you've received input, ask for help in formulating strategies to fix the problem. The more involved employees are, the more committed they'll be to seeing a successful outcome. Involvement is good. Commitment is better!

FAST4

Assess the Workplace Environment on an Ongoing Basis

Swot. Strengths, Weaknesses, Opportunities, Threats. In the simplest of terms, a SWOT analysis is a strategy tool that matches the organization's internal strengths and weaknesses with external opportunities and threats. It's based on the assumption that a careful review of each component of SWOT will produce a strategy to ensure organizational success. Generally, what you're doing is identifying the internal strengths and external opportunities that can be used to overcome internal weaknesses and external threats.

Although you can conduct this analysis alone, it's much better to do it in a group setting. More diverse people give you a more diverse (and accurate) perspective. Let's see how this might work with a workplace issue:

Issue: It takes too long to complete the hiring process, from the time an opening is recognized to the day a job offer is extended.

A SWOT Analysis of this issue might begin to take this form:

STRENGTHS	WEAKNESSES	OPPORTUNITIES	THREATS
Staff has a willingness to review issue and is highly motivated to make positive changes.	Work is often uncoordinated— right hand doesn't know what the left hand is doing.	Two local companies recently had large layoffs—additional people in the labor pool.	Tight, competitive job market.
Good relationships with all internal players.	Poor communication.	Have relationship with an outside consultant that can facilitate the process.	Not attracting high caliber candidates.
All involved are excellent interviewers.	The process has a number of steps viewed as unnecessary.	Outside community views our organization as "world class."	Candidates tell us that they are kept hanging for too long before an offer is made.

As you continue on with the SWOT analysis, you can begin to see how your strengths might be used to overcome your weaknesses and how you can turn those threats into opportunities. One great strength is that the staff has a willingness to review and make changes. This can go a long way in improving the coordination of work and communication systems. The fact that there are good internal relationships and that the community perceives the organization as world class can be used to leverage publicity about the positive work environment, which in turn may be pivotal in being successful in a tight job market.

FAST5

Be a Management Gladiator

I F YOU HAVEN'T SEEN THE MOVIE *GLADIATOR*, I highly recommend renting it for a day or two. The lead character, Maximus, is a Roman general, turned slave, turned gladiator, turned savior of Rome. As general for Caesar's legion, Maximus had the respect and admiration of his followers. As a gladiator, fighting in the arenas that dotted the countryside and finally at the Roman Coliseum, he had the respect and admiration of his fellow gladiators and the crowd. Why? Because he embodied the truest and most basic qualities that people look for in their leaders:

✦ Willingness to lead the task at hand and then work side by side. Maximus did not expect his followers to do anything that he would not do himself. In fact, he took the lead and set the tone. Whether it was fighting Germania or Commodus the Emperor of Rome, he led by example. And he continued to stand next to his men, encouraging them, protecting them and celebrating their successes.

✦ Balance. While Maximus's accomplishments as a general and gladiator would have been plenty, we are constantly reminded of his devotion to his wife, son, gods and country. Maximus worked to keep an enviable balance in his life.

✦ Integrity. All of his decisions were steeped in "doing the right thing." He approached each challenge in his life without self-interest or self-reward.

✦ Belief in a higher calling. All that Maximus did was based on his belief of a better Rome. Each action that he took, including his death, was done to achieve the long-term goal . . . returning Rome to the control of the Senate.

How can you use these four qualities to improve your leadership? Would your employees see these qualities in you? Are you the management gladiator?

FAST6

Be Available

"**W**E'RE PROUD OF THE FACT THAT OUR company practices an open-door policy!" In a recent exit interview, an ex-employee stated, "My manager says that he has an open-door policy, but it's really not true. He thinks an open-door policy is all about seeing us when it's convenient for him, but he's only here two days a week. There are lots of problems that come up when he's not here, and we can't ever find him to discuss them. If we try to handle it on our own, we get disciplined. It's a no-win situation, and that's mostly why I left. If he had made himself more available, maybe I would have stayed."

Available means not only having your door open, but also being visible at the worksite. This might mean having face-to-face conversations, either formally or informally. In this day and age of virtual teams and people that are spread from site to site, sometimes that isn't so easy. You can also be visible to your employees through:

✦ Casual telephone conversations.

✦ E-mail.

✦ Forwarding information, such as memos, articles and other news items of importance.

Let's spend a minute talking about the do's and don'ts for effectively using the above mechanisms.

Phone or E-mail

DO: Casually call or e-mail to see:

✦ How it's going.

✦ To ask for more details on an on-going project.

✦ To positively reinforce good performance.

✦ To ask what you can do to help make their jobs easier.

✦ To brief the employee on new developments in the department or the company.

✦ To check on certain milestones; i.e., project completion

✦ To touch base before or after vacations, weekends, etc.

DON'T: Casually call or email:

✦ To discipline or otherwise chastise an employee for a less than stellar performance.

✦ To blow off steam about anything.

✦ If it looks or sounds like you're being perfunctory.

✦ Using language that isn't 100% acceptable (cursing never is).

DO: Forward information to:

✦ Keep employees in the loop.

✦ Present them with new information that will be useful to their work.

✦ Validate what they are currently working on.

DON'T: Forward information that:

+ Shows them they're doing something incorrectly.
+ Validates your point of view.
+ Is of no value to them.

Inevitably, the question of how to handle sticky situations by phone comes up. Can these be handled by phone? Sometimes that's the only option. When this is the case, schedule time with the employee; don't catch them off guard. Let them know what you want to talk about in advance so that they, too, can prepare for the conversation. Then, when the conversation is over, send the employee a written account so that both of you are on the same sheet of music. Back to FAST1—Address Potentially Sticky Situations Head On.

FAST7

Infuse Passion. . . Be a Naked Manager

IN THE LAST DECADE, CULINARY FINESSE HAS come into vogue. Not since Julia Child and Graham Kerr (the Galloping Gourmet) have the culinary arts been elevated to such a high level. Chefs like Emeril, Bobby Flay, Sarah Moulton and Malto Mario enter our living rooms and our lives on a daily basis. The cream of the newest crop is British chef Jamie Oliver. A mere twenty six years old, he is a best-selling cookbook author, cooking show guru, food editor of the *British GQ* magazine, runs London's trendy River Café and has cooked for the British prime minister. Never heard of him? Perhaps you've heard of "The Naked Chef." That's the name most of us recognize.

As a note, he does not cook in the nude. "Naked" is his self-described cooking style. When Oliver talks about cooking he says, "It's not about rocket science. It's just about passion."

Passion can often be the difference between good and great, between mediocrity and achievement. It can be the difference in what helps you lead your employees to greater levels of performance. Ask yourself these questions:

✦ Do I love my job? If not, do I at least *really* like it? (It's okay not to love or really like fill-in jobs during your early years, but when you're in a position of leading and managing others, this is critical.)

✦ Am I enthusiastic? How do I show it?

✦ How would other people describe my attitude towards my job?

If your answers point to anything less than a high level of enthusiasm and excitement, it might be time for a tune-up. Every job has its fair share of mundane tasks, problems and obstacles, but the best managers don't focus on those. The focus is on what they love about the job; what they are passionate about. And that focus translates into a better work environment.

When the going gets tough, think about what brought you to that job in the first place. Where was your initial passion? How did that job-related passion grow? How can you stoke the fires of passion to get back on track (and yes . . . I think this works for relationships, too . . . although that's another book!)?

FAST8

Be Positively Unpredictable When It Counts

S AME OLD, SAME OLD . . . OR IS IT? AS MAN-
agers, we are drilled in consistency, in treating people
fairly and in having predictable responses. There's good
reason for that. In any organization, employees need to
know that when certain events transpire, there will be predictable responses. We even teach managers how to do this
in classes on behavior modification. It helps to promote an
environment where employees can feel a certain degree of
physical and emotional security. To some extent, that's the
way it should be. Or should it?

Sometimes unpredictability, properly placed, can have
tremendous impact on morale. I'm not talking about
unpredictably chastising employees or unpredictably not
showing up for a scheduled meeting. Good manners and
proper etiquette will always prevail. The type of unpredictability I'm talking about has more to do with cama-
raderie and positive influence.

Try some of these suggestions:

✦ If you're the one who never makes the coffee . . . learn to make it!

✦ If you're the one who rarely has time for lunch . . . bring pizza in for everyone!

✦ If you're the one who takes phone calls during meetings . . . put on the DND (do not disturb)!

✦ If you're the one who waits for employees to come to you for help or advice . . . seek them out *before* they come to you!

✦ If you're the one who always stays late . . . leave on time (and insist that your staff leave, too)!

You get the idea . . . the point is that this unpredictability can be like a breath of fresh air and energize your workforce. Employees certainly notice when you do something out of character, and when it's positive it can have a ripple effect throughout your organization. Employees will often follow your lead, so just a few randomly placed acts of unpredictability can light a flame of enthusiasm and newfound morale.

FAST9

Build Positive Alliances, Even With the Not-So-Positive

I T'S EASY TO WORK WITH THE PLEASANT PEOPLE. It's easy to build relationships and alliances with those that share similar points of view or are just nicer with which to work. But then there's the other side . . . the people that we must work with, but don't like to.

Often our first inclination is to either put up barriers or try to ignore people that we find difficult. Why do we need more difficult people in our lives? However, there is good to be gained by building these alliances. As a supervisor, you can demonstrate the power of building positive alliances and reap the benefits.

+ Look at those that play an integral part in the operation of your department, but are perceived as difficult. What are their strengths? What can you do to capitalize on those strengths?

+ Who can you enlist to help you build alliances? Find the person everyone likes and talk with them. They'll probably be glad to offer you some insight into their relationship success.

How do you go about implementing just one of their insights? Here's an example close to home. At the beginning of my human resource career, I had a boss about whom I felt mostly ambivalent. One day, though, he got my attention, and it was at that point I realized the power he had in building positive alliances.

The company accounting system was undergoing a major change—everything was to be automated. To most people that was a welcome change. After all, keeping manual records was cumbersome and not always accurate. However, the accounting supervisor had a different perspective. She was not at all happy about the impending change and was doing all she could to fight it. She visited my boss regularly to complain about everything that would go wrong with the new system. The complaining was no surprise—the accounting supervisor had a reputation as a "professional complainer." Most of us just wrote her off as not being a team player.

My boss listened to her, and then he said, "It sounds like you have some real concerns. Could you write all of them down for me and get that to me by the end of the week?" What could she say? By the end of the week, my boss had five handwritten (front and back) pages of everything that could possibly go wrong during the conversion. He then went to see the MIS director, handed him a copy of the list and said, "Here's everything that Mary thinks could go wrong. I'd like for both of you to meet to talk about it and see if these items can be addressed."

Fast forward to the end of the story. After several meetings, all of the items had been addressed. The conversion occurred on time. And, it was smooth sailing! You see, my boss capitalized on Mary's strength—her ability to complain! He used that in a way that built a positive alliance. The conversion went off without a hitch, Mary was part of the process and there were no causalities along the way.

FAST 10

Celebrate the Small Stuff

According to *The American Heritage Dictionary of the English Language*, *celebrate* is defined as, "To observe (a day or event) with ceremonies of respect, festivity, or rejoicing; to perform (a religious ceremony); to extol or praise; to make widely known; display; to engage in festivities."

We all know what it's like to "engage in festivities." We engage in festivities when we celebrate employee anniversaries and birthdays, successfully completed projects and individual and team achievements. We display our pride on "Walls of Fame" that feature employees of the month and other organizational achievers. Senior leadership may frequently extol or praise employees from the podium at an organization-wide meeting.

That covers the big stuff, but what about the smaller, everyday stuff? Here's where "ceremonies of respect" come into play.

Usually when we think about ceremonies of respect, we immediately think of religious ceremonies, swearing-in ceremonies or something similar. Again, this is the big stuff. There are opportunities every day for you to fashion your own personal ceremonies of respect, and use them to reinforce the daily small stuff that so often slips through the cracks. Here are a few suggestions to get you started on developing and maintaining your own ceremonies of respect:

✦ Look for something that will be the "tie that binds" with your employees. For example, could you have a weekly or monthly lunch, for no other reason than to say, "Thank you for being here every day." Be sensitive to employee needs and desires. Just a note - celebrating a weekly lunch with pizza is fine, but not if someone is lactose intolerant! Be aware of dietary restrictions.

✦ Involve your employees in developing rituals and traditions. You might be surprised with their ideas, especially the simplicity. For example, one secretary, given the opportunity to fashion a ritual, decided that a ten-minute cup of coffee with her boss each morning was important to her. The intent? It was nothing more than to get the day off to a good start and to build the personal relationship. The time he took with her said, "I respect you enough and think you're important enough to spend time with you (*and I won't ask you to type a memo!*)." No cost, but a big payout.

✦ Keep it up! Nothing screams fad of the month more loudly than a good intention that gets swept under the carpet. It's up to you to ensure that these small celebrations become an integral part of your work environment.

FAST11

Delegate, Enrich and Empower

"THE PEOPLE'S CAPACITY TO ACHIEVE IS determined by their leader's ability to empower" stated by John Maxwell in *The 21 Irrefutable Laws of Leadership*. Good leaders figure out how to delegate meaningful tasks to enrich an employee's job. Enrichment does not mean enlargement. And indiscriminate "task dumping" is just that—job enlargement. Good managers are deliberate and think carefully before delegating. Strong leaders take this one step further and empower employees to achieve their goals. This is not an easy task. Too often, for fear of project or personal failure, leaders meddle with the means and undercut the employee in their quest for empowerment.

"It would take so long to teach someone,
that I might as well do it myself."

There is some truth to that statement. In our busy environments, we have a tendency to focus on what needs to be done immediately. What usually needs to be done NOW can be most quickly accomplished by doing it ourselves. However, as supervisors, not only are we responsible for getting the work done, but we are responsible for developing the people that report to us. Delegation is one of the ways we develop staff skills and lay the foundation for an empowered workforce.

Delegation serves several purposes:

◆ Helps you to better manage not only your time, but the time of those people that report to you.

◆ Provides learning opportunities, which leads to empowered employees.

◆ Allows you to reallocate work so that you can focus on the most important areas

Here are six tips for effective delegation—*that enriches, not enlarges*—the job!

◆ Identify what work can be delegated. If you have identified something that cannot be delegated, ask yourself why.

◆ Be familiar with the background, skills, credentials and capabilities of the person that will be performing the delegated work.

◆ Make sure that you are available (especially in the beginning) to answer questions. If there are opportunities for the person to make independent decisions, let him or her know. If you will not be available, have another person act as your back up.

◆ Be clear in your communications. How does the person best relate to information? Be prepared to present instructions using a variety of methods. Use active listening skills to check for understanding.

◆ Establish process checks or checkpoints to review progress.

◆ Give constructive feedback to modify or continue performance.

FAST 12

Encourage Community Involvement, Tap into the Energy

Iᶠ ʏᴏᴜ ᴡᴀɴᴛ ᴛᴏ ꜰɪɴᴅ ᴏᴜᴛ ᴡʜᴇʀᴇ ʏᴏᴜʀ employees' enthusiasm and true talents lie, just look at what they do outside of work. Every community benefits from the volunteers that give their time, energy and money to a vast array of non-profit agencies, religious groups and youth activities. They are coaches; participants in walk-a-thons, marathons and telethons; tutors; envelope stuffers; board members; book readers; clean-up crews; and house builders. The list goes on and on. While the activities are as diverse as the people themselves, they all have one thing in common. Giving their talents for a greater good.

How do you harness that enthusiasm
and talent in the workplace?

Generally, people give of themselves outside the work-place because they get some intrinsic level of satisfaction. It taps into one or more of their "Engines of Motivation." Some of those engines are: Engine of Ownership, Engine of

Significance, Engine of Belonging, Engine of Recognition, Engine of Achievement, Engine of Power and Authority and Engine of Competency (based on Dean Spitzer's *Super-Motivation*, Amacon, 1995). We are all driven to some degree by one, and sometimes several, of these engines.

The trick, of course, is to find out which engine(s) is driving which person. Although motivation is a very individual thing, here's what you can immediately do:

✦ Ask each employee if they're involved in outside activities, and if so, which ones.

✦ Ask each employee why he or she is involved and what they get out of that activity.

✦ Ask them what special skills or talents they use during the community activity that they're not able to use on the job.

✦ Ask if they would like to be able to use more of those talents on the job.

✦ Ask if they would like to work together to develop a plan to utilize more of the talents they've described.

FAST13

Es Es (or Eat, Eat)

FOOD PROVIDES A POWERFUL BOND, AND IN many cultures food is inextricably linked to sharing events. Weddings, funerals, birthdays, retirements, religious services, and even the Super Bowl, are events that are built around food. Food is associated with fellowship and sharing. It not only feeds our bodies, it also fuels our souls. Events and rituals built around food and work can also improve the workplace environment.

One company uses food as a means of furthering their commitment and understanding of diversity issues. Each week features a specific type of lunch. For example, this week might be Mexican, next week Japanese, the week after Jamaican, the next week Native American and so forth, until each culture represented in the company has been highlighted. Food is either purchased or brought in by employees. After everyone has served themselves, a brief program is conducted that highlights that particular culture. It might be a video, a lecture or discussion or a skit. The point is, people have an opportunity to enjoy good food, fellowship and learn something that is important to their organization's culture.

Another company sponsors a "Lunch and Learn" session each month. Pizza or sandwiches are available at no charge to employees. While eating, a professional development topic is presented that is of interest to the group. It might be on communications, presentation skills or how to better manage conflict. The lunch gives people an opportunity to meet and learn in a relaxed environment.

A supervisor at another company was working under a tight deadline to get a mailing out. She told her secretary to hold all her calls and that she was not to be disturbed because the mailing had to be finalized. It looked like an extraordinarily long night. After a few minutes, her secretary knocked on the door. She said that she had talked to everyone in the department, and all but one would stay late to help get the mailing out. As it was, everyone was at the office until about 8:00 p.m. About 5:00 p.m., the supervisor made a call and had pizzas brought in. This proved to be the proverbial icing on the cake. Working and eating, the job got done in a congenial, warm atmosphere.

Look for opportunities. How can you use food to help improve your work environment? Not sure? Ask your employees! They will most certainly give you suggestions that can be immediately used!

FAST14

Find Opportunities to Collaborate with Other Departments, Units, etc.

I N A RECENT SURVEY AT A LARGE COMPANY, employees rated relationships in their own teams or departments as very positive. However, when it came to relationships with other departments, the rating was downright negative. Additionally, the employees that were surveyed felt that these negative relationships were preventing them from doing the best job possible. When asked what was being done to improve the situation, not one person could identify a single, tangible action.

The truth is, most of us do not operate in a vacuum. No person is an island, and that goes double for departments and work teams. We not only rely on people in our own departments, but often we must share critical information with people in other departments, divisions, worksites and even outside the organization. Too busy to forge relationships with everyone? Try this process to get started:

1. Identify the critical work processes that your department must perform (remember to involve everyone in the department).
2. Identify which functions go outside of your department.
   ✦ What information is passed on by your department?
   ✦ What information is received by your department?
3. What is the relationship with the department on the giving/receiving end? (Use a 1–5 rating, 1 meaning the relationship is abysmal, 5 meaning that the relationship is terrific.)
4. For all those receiving a 1, 2, or 3 prioritize how important that department is in your work processes.
5. Develop an action plan, one department or person at a time. For example, in one company, the human resources department must often interface with the finance department. The HR Department rated the relationships with accounts payable and payroll as a "2." The action plan looked something like this:

STEP NUMBER	ACTION	PEOPLE RESPONSIBLE	DONE BY
1	Department heads meet to discuss the situation, develop a schedule, and agree on outcomes and goals.	HR Director/ Controller	April 1
2	Meeting is scheduled to discuss concerns and how the work relationships can be improved. All departments are separately briefed so that everyone has the same understanding.	HR Director/ Controller responsible for arranging for people in applicable departments to be present.	April 15
3	Meeting occurs. At the meeting specific actionable items are agreed on, including an evaluation mechanism.	Department employees, with oversight from management.	April 22
4	Follow up occurs to ensure that all actionable items are occurring.	Department employees, with oversight from management.	Through June 1
5	Assess progress on goals (evaluation mechanism) to assess improvement.	Department employees, with oversight from management.	June 7
6	Meet again to review progress.	Department employees, with oversight from management.	June 10

FAST 15

Find Out What Motivates Employees, and Then Use It

Y OU MAY HAVE READ *THE ADVENTURES OF Tom Sawyer* by Mark Twain. In the book, we read about Aunt Polly's demand that Tom whitewash the fence. It was a glorious Saturday and, like most youngsters, Tom had other plans. When the other children found out that Tom had to work, they made fun of him, ridiculing him for having to do distasteful chores.

A youngster might be sad or, at the very least, miffed because the other kids were free to play. A youngster might also be upset being the object of ridicule.

But not Tom Sawyer!

As the story goes, Tom convinced the other children that it was great fun to whitewash the fence . . . so much fun that by the end of the day the youngsters were *paying* Tom to participate in this once ridiculed activity. What did Tom do to motivate the youngsters? He tapped into those engines of motivation!

Consider these motivation engines (based on Dean Spitzer's *Super-Motivation*, Amacon, 1995):

Engine of Ownership

People have an innate desire to possess tangible (and intangible) goods. Very often, we measure our self-worth by what we own, such as our home, vehicle, clothing or jewelry. We take pride in those things that we consider to be ours. The same is true with intangibles, such as values and ideas. Think about how you felt the last time someone disagreed with you or criticized a closely held belief. Employees have the same desire to own their jobs—materials, ideals, and the work they produce.

Engine of Significance

We want what we do to be deemed important. We want it to be meaningful and to make a difference. We want to have an impact on those who are important to us. We want our endeavors to be worthy. This is often done through charity work or through social or religious causes. Imagine if that energy could be unleashed at the workplace. As supervisors, as managers, we need to find outlets at work to help our employees find their work meaningful and significant.

Engine of Belonging

Human beings are social by nature and want to belong to a group. This is seen at college campuses with fraternities and sororities, community service organizations like Rotary and Kiwanis, and groups like the Shriners. We see numerous groups at senior centers, bowling leagues and professionally oriented groups. The workplace provides critical contact and opportunities for socializing and relationship building. In fact, for some, work is *the* social cornerstone.

Engine of Recognition and Achievement

Nothing succeeds like success! Achievement is success, and achievement breeds more achievement. People like to achieve at the workplace. Achievement is usually the product of hard work, determination and/or perseverance. The very fact that someone has achieved something brings a feeling of pride and accomplishment from within. However, it's also important that others, particularly supervisors in the workplace, recognize those accomplishments. All of us want to be sincerely appreciated for the contributions we make.

Engine of Power and Authority

Although the desire for power and authority is rooted in human nature, when given the opportunity to obtain it, we often turn the other way. Empowerment is a term we hear today, yet employees often act as if they do not want be empowered. We naturally resist external control (remember rebellious teenagers), yet when given the opportunity to exercise control, we are reticent to take it. Why? Organizational structure. The organization very much dictates what we can and cannot do. There are policies and procedures, guidelines and regulations.

Engines of Competency

Virtually all human beings want to feel as if they are good at something. We want to skillfully master tasks through self-learning and learning from others. It is by gaining competence that we develop self-esteem—the feeling that we are truly capable and skillful.

How can you tap into one or more of these engines to help spark motivation in your workforce?

FAST 16

Give Credit

THERE IS A TELEVISION SHOW CALLED "JUDGING Amy." The program is about the trials and tribulations of a family-court judge and her family. In one episode she decides to organize an adoption day. She brings the idea to her boss, the "head judge," who poo-poo's the idea. However, he says if she can get the other judges on board, which means volunteering their time on a Saturday, she can do it. She talks to the other judges and they reluctantly agree. Fast forward to the Saturday adoption day. The hallowed halls of the courthouse are crammed with families. We see Amy enter, drenched from a torrential storm, only to cast her eyes on her boss, who is talking to the press. With a baby in one arm, he extols the virtues of the day and handily takes full credit for the idea and implementation.

What does Judge Amy Gray do? After hearing from her CSO that she should set the record straight, she looks at him and says that she won't do that. It's enough that the day came together.

The point is, Judge Gray was willing to set aside her own ego for the greater good of the program success and that others were benefiting from her efforts. Where are the opportunities that you can set aside your own desire for recognition to ensure that your employees receive it?

Take a look at these opportunities:

+ At meetings.
+ At breaks.
+ At lunch.
+ While talking to a third party.
+ During informal performance reviews.
+ Formally—on a bulletin board, at a formal recognition program or similar event.
+ In an article, memo or other written piece.
+ On camera.
+ Off the record.

Giving credit where credit is due returns dedicated, loyal employees.

FAST17

Use SIMPLE Feedback

Feedback is the breakfast of champions! —Rick Tate

T HERE'S NOTHING LIKE CONSTRUCTIVE FEEDBACK for improving and changing employee performance. For organizations looking for a big return on investment . . . well . . . look no further. This is it! Feedback costs nothing. Anyone can give and receive it at almost any time. And, done correctly, it has far-reaching and long-lasting results.

For feedback to be truly effective, keep it **SIMPLE.**

Sensitive

Start establishing relationships by respecting people's sensitivities. When giving feedback, this means being aware of the issues and buttons that help and hinder effective feedback. For example, if the person that you're giving feedback to is hypersensitive or overly emotional, consider saving the discussion for the end of the day, and preferably on a Friday. That way, the person has an opportunity to think about what's been discussed, and if it's less-than-favorable, there is opportunity to regain one's composure and not have to face an office full of inquiring minds. Also, think about the different sensitivities that come from diverse cultural backgrounds. There are also different perceptions based on age, gender, ethnic and religious background, sexual orientation and race. Consider those factors when giving feedback.

Issue Related

If you're looking to give feedback on a specific subject, make sure that it's just that . . . specific! Keep it relevant to the issue at hand and don't load on other stuff. If you want the person to focus, then it's important for you to focus, too. Resist the urge to cover just one more thing.

Meaningful

Can the person take action on the feedback you're giving? For example, an employee may have a problem getting to work on time. If the feedback is designed to reaffirm the company's attendance policy and get the employee's commitment to be on time, you may be missing the mark. If the root of the problem is that the school bus comes late each morning and the employee cannot leave until the school bus has picked up her first-grader, then the feedback needs to be designed to address the issue at hand—the school bus schedule and how the work schedule might be flexed. Getting feedback on areas where you can exercise little or no control only leads to frustration.

Prompt

Feedback is best given shortly after the event that triggers the need for feedback. If the employee has done something well, don't wait until the quarterly review to mention it; likewise if performance problems need correction. Frequent, sincere and applicable feedback helps to promote an environment of open and honest communication. There's no time like the present! And, remember to use feedback for the positive as well as the developmental area.

Listen

Although by the very act of giving feedback you're the one speaking, you can make feedback more effective by making it two-way. Use active listening skills, both attending and reflecting. Be aware of body language and use repetition and paraphrasing. Check for understanding, and let the person that you're talking with know that you really understand the core of his or her message.

Easy to Understand

Use words, analogies and examples that are easily understood. Be careful of jargon or slang. If the person has a different cultural background, be aware of language that might be misinterpreted. Use neuro-linguistic programming (NLP) to help others take in and process information more effectively. If the person is more visual (processes information best by seeing), write things down, use pictures or flip charts. If the person is more auditory (processes information best by hearing), make sure that there is lots of two-way discussion. If the person is kinesthetic (processes information best by doing), think about using role-plays or games to emphasize a point.

FAST 18

What I Like About You

F ROM TIME TO TIME, WHEN I'M WORKING WITH a group over a five-day period, tensions can mount and emotions run high, especially if the group is in unfamiliar territory. Although groups do come together, and make progress, it's sometimes difficult to remember that there was once enjoyment in working together. To bring a group or team together, and to reinforce the positive, I lead the group through the following exercise:

1. Each person receives as many sheets of paper as there are people in the group.
2. Envelopes are placed on a separate table with each person's name on an envelope (one envelope per person).
3. The back of each person's chair is labeled with their name.
4. I then ask each person to think about the best qualities of each person. Each person chooses three best qualities.
5. Each member of the group then uses a separate sheet of paper for each person, puts the name on top, and writes down those three best qualities. (This is where

the labeled chairs come in handy . . . not everyone remembers everyone's name.)

6. No one signs his or her name; this is an anonymous exercise.

7. At the completion of the exercise, all slips are handed to me and I place them into each person's envelope. (I do read the notes before placing them in the envelope to ensure that the spirit of the exercise is carried out properly.)

8. I then seal the envelopes and at the end of the session, I distribute them to the participants.

As you might expect, the participants race to their cars to tear open the envelopes. It's not unusual for one or two to come back into the room, or to call me in a few days and say thank you for a great send-off. How can you adapt this to send-off your team with a positive note?

FAST 19

Involve Employees in Decision Making Whenever Possible

D URING EXIT INTERVIEWS, AN INTERESTING piece of information that often comes out is that employees do not feel their input is considered in decision making. It's not unusual to hear employees say that although they have the authority to make small decisions to get their job done, when it comes to decisions that have a major impact on their work lives, they aren't asked for input. Furthermore, they also state that they do not understand the reasoning behind many of the decisions that are made.

Think about it. Here's an opportunity to build relationships and to enhance the level of employee commitment. It doesn't cost anything. A person with a hand in the design phase is much more likely to be committed to seeing it through to a successful outcome. If we want to build a committed workforce, it would stand to reason that you'd ask for employee input and then act on that input whenever possible.

You may say that it's too time consuming; there are other, more important things you must work on. Could one of those more important things be hiring new staff? What a waste! Here's a way to get started:

1. Sit down and make a list of the most important decisions that need to be made in your department (or business unit, division, etc.).

2. Look at the staff you have and decide which areas they could have the most positive impact. In the beginning, go for the quick win.

3. Call your group together:

   ✦ Explain that you'd like their input on whatever area you've chosen.

   ✦ Give them whatever background information they'll need.

   ✦ Specifically state what you want as the outcome or goal. Quantify. (We need to reduce processing time by 7 days.)

   ✦ Outline any parameters. (Can't cost more than x, must be stand alone, etc.)

   ✦ Make the resources they'll need available to them. (time, money, materials, etc.)

   ✦ Give the group a general time frame, but let them develop the time line.

4. Answer any questions they have and be prepared to offer assistance whenever needed.

It is important for you to commit to using the group's suggestions. If you are effectively facilitating the group, what they come up with shouldn't surprise you. Although this process may be a bit more time consuming in the beginning, the payback is tenfold. You're building a self-sufficient, self-directed team. That's a powerful force in an exceptional work environment.

FAST20

Involve Employees in the Hiring Process

W<small>HEN</small> I'M <small>LOOKING TO HIRE MORE PEOPLE AND</small> I have a high performing person working with me, the first thing I ask is, "Anymore like you?" Chances are, the people they recommend have the same great work ethic. I also ask people that work with me to get involved in the process. It might involve assessing a resume, sitting with someone and conducting a realistic job preview, or participating in the interview. There are many opportunities for involvement.

Here are my "Top Ten Ways to Involve Employees in the Hiring Process":

1. Have employees determine the behaviors that are needed to perform the job (that you're hiring for) successfully. They can gather firsthand information and ask other job incumbents and managers. The output of this is a list of five to ten characteristics a person needs in order to be successful in that job.

2. Involve employees in writing the interview questions based on the characteristics identified in #1.

3. Involve employees in the actual interview process, with a defined, substantive role. This means actively participating, not just observing.

4. Delegate writing the interview summaries, and any scoring that might go along with the summaries. For example, you may score applicants on the way they answer each behavior-based question.

5. Establish criteria for prescreening resumes or applications, and then let the employees do that.

6. Have employees write the ads that are placed in the newspaper or professional journal.

7. Have employees spend a few hours conducting a realistic job preview. (This is a true-to-life explanation or demonstration of what the job is really about.)

8. Employees can do reference checks. With a little bit of training, it's an educational exercise.

9. Choose one employee as the "Point Person." This is the person that coordinates all activities related to the interviewing process.

10. Have the employee contact all of the people that were not offered the job (but were interviewed). Have them establish a personal relationship by phoning. If someone made it as far as the interview process, you want to keep the door open for future opportunities.

FAST 21

Hold Yourself to the Highest Standards

Athough this seems obvious, in this day and age of "standards of convenience," it bears repeating. Employees buy into the person first, then the vision. You can't expect employees to have the highest standards if you do not. Employees first care about what you do, not what you say. Although you may be able to cite examples where this is the contrary (and who doesn't remember Bill Clinton's sexcapades), for most of us, this is just not the case.

Employees look at us with a critical eye, which gives us the opportunity to lead by example. Some years ago, I was a human resources manager, and one of my responsibilities was to develop and conduct soft-skill training programs. One such program that was done was on effective communications. Effective communication is of utmost importance in building a great workplace. The program was attended by all management staff and generally received high marks and much praise.

A few weeks after the program, one of the participants came roaring into my office and demanded to speak with me immediately. My body language showed obvious annoyance and I said with a combination sweet/sarcastic voice that surely I was doing nothing all day but waiting for them to let me know what my priorities should be. We both looked at each other and then had a good laugh. I figured the air was cleared. However, a week after that, I received some disturbing feedback: "You may be able to teach communications, but you sure couldn't do what you teach."

That was upsetting, to say the least. And the most interesting thing was that if I had 99 interactions with this person, they would all be good. It was the one that caught me off-guard and where I responded in a less than professional manner, that came back to hurt my credibility. One out of 100. The 99 successful interactions only held my credibility within the status quo. The one unsuccessful interaction caused a meltdown.

Here are four things to remember when holding yourself to the highest standards:

1. Know what your standard is and know what behaviors you can visibly demonstrate so employees will know beyond a shadow of a doubt the standard you adhere to.
2. Base all your interactions in the interest of upholding your standard(s).
3. Understand what is important to your people. They need to be able to easily identify with the standards you're communicating, not only through what you say but also through what you do.
4. If you falter (and you will from time to time), do damage control. Fess up! Recognition that you've fallen from the standard is powerful—everyone else knows it . . . they need to know that you know it, too.

FAST22

Communicate for Understanding

ACH ONE OF US HAS PREFERRED WAYS OF
communicating; that is, expressing our thoughts and
taking in and processing information. The five senses are
the representational systems in neuro-linguistic programming (NLP): visual, auditory, kinesthetic, gustatory and
olfactory. These senses represent what we see, hear, touch
or feel, taste, and smell. Interestingly, these systems come
into play during our everyday communications. The most
common are auditory (how we hear things), visual (how
we see things) and kinesthetic (how we feel and touch
things). For example, if you asked your employees for an
opinion on a new attendance policy, they might respond in
the following manner:

> Visual person: I can see both sides of implementing it.
>
> Auditory person: I've heard that there might be prob-
> lems with people accepting it.
>
> Kinesthetic person: I don't feel that it will help improve
> attendance.

Understanding how to present information can greatly enhance communications. Since it is often difficult to determine what someone's preferred method of taking in and processing information might be, it's important to offer information that touches on all modalities. For example:

To capitalize on visual senses: Offer information in writing by using notes, memos, letters, written agendas, flip charts, overheads, PowerPoint or workbooks.

To capitalize on auditory senses: Offer information verbally through two-way discussion—either face to face, by telephone or using web technology, tapes or CDs or lectures.

To capitalize on kinesthetic senses: Offer information that involves the person in the design, use simulations, role-play, case studies, what-if scenarios or games.

Once you figure out how to best present the information, always check for understanding by using reflecting skills. These include repetition and paraphrasing. Repetition merely gives the person back what they've said to you in their words. Paraphrasing allows you to restate what the person has said, putting it in your words. This lets the other person know that you understand the core message . . . which is critical when crystal clear communication is needed.

FAST23

Have a Vision, Take Action

I_N J_{OEL} B_{ARKER'S} 1991 _{VIDEO,} "T_{HE} P_{OWER OF} Vision," he makes the following statement: "Vision without action is merely a dream. Action without vision just passes the time. Vision with action can change the world." How true.

Your vision manifests itself in a philosophical statement that describes the possible future you see for your department or business unit. It describes the department and its impact on the future and is guided by possibilities and dreams, not constraints. Vision statements are inspirational and give all those affiliated (both internally and externally) with the department something to grab and hold onto. Everything that the department does flows from the vision. And of course, the department's vision statement directly flows from the organization's (if there is one).

This is not to be confused with mission. Mission statements are also philosophical and include the need (values-based) that the department fulfills in the organization and what the department does to meet that need. Mission statements are *brief* and can be easily remembered and internalized by department members. If your organization has a mission statement, yours should flow from that.

What is the vision for your department or business unit? Here are some easy steps to follow to start generating your vision statement:

1. Start by involving everyone in your department. A short brainstorming session is a good starting point and should be done round-robin fashion so that everyone participates. Generate as many ideas as possible on what main themes should be included in the vision. This is not the time to wordsmith . . . there will be plenty of time for that later!

2. After you've exhausted all ideas, review the list to clarify any ideas that may not be clearly understood by everyone in the group. Then combine similar ideas, and eliminate items on the list that are no longer applicable.

3. Use either weighted voting or nominal group technique to determine consensus on the top three or four ideas.

4. Take those top ideas and break into small groups (if the group is large), and come up with a sentence that captures that idea.

5. Put all of the sentences together and start wordsmithing.

6. Voila! You have a vision statement!

After the vision statement is accepted by all members of the department, it should act as your compass, giving guidance and direction to all that you do. The vision statement should be reviewed at least once a year to determine if it still makes sense.

FAST24

Go to Bat

W ITHOUT A DOUBT, BUILDING TRUST AND loyalty in your workforce is a never-ending and difficult job. However, what helps clear the path for an environment of trust is the knowledge that you, as manager, will speak up for your people when they're not able to speak for themselves. This is relatively easy to do when praise is involved. It becomes far more difficult when someone is looking to lay blame for a project or a decision that has run amok.

There are many instances when you'll have the opportunity to go to bat for your team, department or any one of the employees that works for you. Some instances are:

✦ For an innovative or markedly different way of doing something.

✦ To justify why someone has been assigned to a specific task.

✦ To justify a position in your department.

✦ To give praise to something being done that the rest of the organization has not noticed.

✦ To ask for additional resources to enable people to do a better job.

✦ To answer for a poorly made decision.

✦ To explain why a project is off-track.

You get the idea . . . and you probably have dozens more! Use any and all of these situations to get behind your team or employee, to fully show your support when they are not able. Make a point to have a mental checklist ready so that when the opportunity presents itself, you can readily speak on behalf of those that report to you. And, make sure they know about it. Let your people know that the subject came up (it's not necessary to let them know every negative comment that others might have spoken), and what you had to say about it. Use it as an opportunity to reinforce that you think they're doing well and to correct what's not being done well. Most of all, let them know that you are behind them 100% and you're ready, willing, and able to let others know the extent of your support.

FAST25

Eliminate All Types of Harassment

As we ended the 1990s, companies found more and more emphasis being placed on eliminating workplace harassment. In fact, some states mandate anti-harassment training. Whether the harassment is sexual, racial, gender-based, or specific to any other type of protected characteristic, one thing is sure . . . the penalties for not addressing potential and actual situations is substantial. While three of the four Supreme Court decisions of the term that ended in June 1998 gave some guidance (Faragher v. Boca Raton, Burlington Industries, Inc. v. Ellerth, Oncale v. Sundowner Offshore Services, Inc.), organizations still had to wade into many gray areas.

Harassment comes in many forms, from innocent bantering, to pictures, jokes, and actual physical contact, to exchanging favors for job-related benefits. As a supervisor, it's important that you set an environment where all types of harassment are strictly taboo, even those that are unintentional. Guidelines to help you promote a harassment-free environment are:

✦ Lead by example. Be mindful of what you say and do.

✦ Take appropriate measures to stop harassing behavior.

✦ Provide employees with guidelines of what is acceptable and unacceptable behavior, as per your company policy.

✦ Comply with your organization's stated policy.

✦ Provide answers to employee questions, or find out if you don't know.

✦ Keep written records of any incidences (document, document, document).

✦ Keep human resources or the person or department that oversees this area informed. Forward all documentation to them.

When addressing harassment situations, it's not unusual to be viewed as the bad guy, particularly if you've asked people to refrain from certain language or types of jokes. However, it's far better to be a temporary bad guy than to be embroiled in a major problem six months down the road. If you clearly spell out your intentions; that is, provide employees with the best possible working environment, you may even see your staff take up the anti-harassment cause.

FAST26

Help Raise Your Employee's EQ . . . and Yours Too!

FOR MENSA-LIKE SCHOLARS, THE NEWS IS NOT good. EQ is quickly replacing IQ as the hot commodity skill. You can help your employers and employees by raising EQ. What is EQ? It's your emotional intelligence quotient, which results in emotional competency.

Emotional intelligence is a combination of social skills, social awareness, self-awareness, and self-management, and your ability to use these qualities in a positive way when interacting with others. In short, it's the ability to control and express your emotions, and can encompass a wide breadth of personality-type traits.

Reams of research are available on this subject. Daniel Goleman, Ph.D. defines emotional competency as "a learned capability based on emotional intelligence that results in outstanding performance at work." Goleman is the author of several books, most notably his 1995 book titled *Emotional intelligence.* (Admittedly, there are people who are in disagreement with Goleman.)

This concept has significant implications for management and employees alike. If you're management, this can fundamentally change how you hire and develop people. Suddenly, EQ becomes more important than task knowledge. This may change the way interviews are done, job descriptions are written, performance is evaluated, and promotions and pay increases are given. The training focus shifts from hard skills to soft skills.

For your employees, EQ may change how they view their role in the organization and what they need to accomplish in order to maintain or change career paths. Everyday interactions and communications take on added value. Skills such as problem solving, conflict management, ability to handle change, and working in small project teams has greater value in the career equation.

The bottom line is that there is data to support that people with higher EQs are more successful in the workplace. Cary Cherniss, Ph.D., from the Rutgers Graduate School of Applied and Professional Psychology, published a paper that found the following examples of EQ successes (there were 15 more examples):

1. A consulting firm assessed experienced partners on a variety of emotional intelligence competencies. Partners scoring above the median on 9 or more of the 20 competencies delivered $1.2 million more profit from their accounts than did other partners—a 139% incremental gain (Boyatzis, R. E. (1999). From a presentation to the Linkage Conference on Emotional Intelligence, Chicago, IL, September 27, 1999.

2. At a national furniture retailer, salespeople hired based on emotional competence had half the dropout rate during their first year (Hay/McBer Research and Innovation Group, 1997).

3. Research by the Center for Creative Leadership has found that the primary causes of derailment in executives involve deficits in emotional competence. The three primary ones are difficulty in handling change, not being able to work well in a team, and poor interpersonal relations.

So, if you're looking to take yourself, your employees, and the organization to the next level . . . work smarter, not harder, and increase those EQ points!

FAST 27

Grin, Sin and Have Some Fun

Most of us are familiar with Hooters, an establishment known for the "Hooters Girls." At a Panama City Beach Hooters, the manager held a contest in April 2001 to see who could sell the most beer. The top selling waitresses from each area Hooters were entered into a drawing for a new Toyota. (Most of us would be very pleased about that kind of reward and recognition!)

Waitress Jodee Berry was announced the winner. She was taken blindfolded into the parking lot, eagerly anticipating her new car. The blindfold was removed, and before her was a new . . . Toy Yoda. For her efforts, she was the proud owner of a Star Wars Yoda doll. Needless to say, Berry was not amused, although she reports that her manager was inside the restaurant laughing. In fact, she quit her job a week later and sued, alleging fraudulent misrepresentation and breach of contract. What is she looking for? The cost of a new Toyota.

We hear from experts (and non-experts, too!) that we should make our organizations more fun. In fact, programs like FiSH! (from the book *FiSH! A Remarkable Way to Boost Morale and Improve Results*, by Steven Lundin, Ph.D, Harry Paul and John Christensen) are taking the workplace by storm. Two of the major points in the FiSH! program are to Choose Your Attitude and Play. In the context of FiSH!, this is great, especially if you're looking to capture the synergy of your workforce and channel it towards better teamwork, customer service, and profitability.

The problem starts when the "fun" isn't fun for everyone. It really comes back to treating employees fairly and ethically, and building a workplace culture steeped in trust and integrity. It starts with the manager, or highest-ranking senior leader, and trickles down throughout the entire organization.

Grinning and sinning (otherwise known as "having some fun") is a wonderful plus in any workplace. To make sure that it doesn't get too out of hand, be aware of the following guidelines:

Do's:

+ To gauge what is acceptable, ask employees. Involve them in the process.

+ Good, clean fun is almost always in style. If you don't believe me, just look at comedians like Sinbad and Bill Cosby.

+ Self-deprecating humor is usually okay, as long as it's not taken to the extreme.

+ People should feel good about having fun. Watch for smiles.

+ Be a leader in having fun. Special theme days, department lunches, and Secret Santas need to have your participation.

Don'ts:

✦ Offensive, off-color, or otherwise questionable conduct is never acceptable.

✦ Watch the body language reaction of others. Often people won't say that a comment, joke or behavior is bothersome, but their body language may indicate otherwise. Watch for changes in body posture, eye contact, facial expression, and participation in the conversation. These could signal unwelcome behavior.

✦ Don't encourage anything that you wouldn't want on the front page of the newspaper.

✦ Participation from everyone may come slowly. Don't rush or require people to participate. They'll eventually become involved when it appears to be more fun to be involved that not to be involved.

✦ Jokes or humor directed at others should be avoided.

Remember, employees will take their cues from you!

FAST28

Develop Leaders, Not Followers

Ⅰn the workplace, we talk about developing leadership skills, but it seems reserved mostly for managers. Being a manager doesn't automatically bestow upon you leadership status, although it's a good bet that you stand a better chance of being put in the leadership role if you are in the management ranks. An opportunity we miss is to develop leadership skills in the employees that report to us.

When we develop selected managers, we are literally taking baby steps in the leadership cycle. However, when we teach leaders how to develop leaders, we take the proverbial quantum leap.

In *The 21 Irrefutable Laws of Leadership*, author John Maxwell talks about The Law of Explosive Growth (Law 20). Maxwell says, "You will go to the highest level only if you begin developing leaders instead of followers." He then talks about leader's math. With leader's math, the equation becomes simple. For example, for every follower you add, you reap a relative increase in the growth of your organization. Ten good followers give you the power of ten good people. For every leader you add, you not only have the power that leader brings to the table but also the power of the followers and leaders he or she influences. The addition of ten good leaders results in exponential growth, all for the same effort as developing followers!

What does this mean to your organization? Focus on not only teaching leadership skills, but also on teaching your leaders how to teach leadership skills to their employees. This is a good place to start, but as Randall White, Philip Hodgeson, and Stuart Crainer wrote in *The Future of Leadership*, "The rapid rise, and fall, of companies has shown that one good idea will get you going, but a succession of good ideas is needed to keep you in business." So it goes with keeping your business in leaders. Here are a few things to think about:

✦ Leadership development takes resources. Do you have the resources to devote? Can you afford not to devote the resources to gain exponential growth and a competitive advantage?

✦ Is your organization ready to shift its focus; to change the culture into one that expects leadership from all?

✦ What role will the CEO and all senior leadership have instilling this throughout the organization?

✦ What measurable outcomes will you put into place . . . how will you know that your foray into leaders leading leaders has been successful?

To take that quantum leap in your own career, develop leadership skills in others.

FAST 29

Use Recognition That Works

SAY GOOD-BYE TO "EMPLOYEE OF THE MONTH." Bid a fond adieu to five-year pins. Name in the newsletter? Auf wiedersehen and good night! Do you think that's all employees need to feel recognized? If so, it's time to think again!

It is critical for organizations to retain top talent, now more than ever. One way is through individual recognition. Recognizing employees en masse has become routine, watered-down, and in the words of one manager, "Ho-hum."

At a management seminar, we were discussing best practices for rewarding and recognizing employees. The inevitable question was posed. *"Just what is the best way to recognize employees?"* Gathering all the wisdom of the past 20 years, I answered, *"It all depends."* Of course the person that asked the question wanted to know what "it" was dependent upon. My answer: *"Dependent on the individual employee."*

I then asked each person to list his or her employees and how each employee liked to be recognized. Not one person could definitively answer that question. How do you find out? The answer is deceptively simple.

Ask. Involve. Check. Ask again. And again.

Bob Nelson, author of several best-selling books, including *1001 Ways to Reward Employees*, made the following comment regarding recognition. "Raise the awareness of your managers about the importance of them appreciating their employees on a daily basis when they do good work—one-on-one or via voice mail, in writing or e-mail, in meetings . . . The rewards that are most beneficial to any employee are the ones they want! Find out what those might be by asking them in one or more ways. It very well may not be "stuff" at all, but perhaps autonomy, flexibility, trust, support, visibility, opportunity, and so forth."

Start by asking your employees what's meaningful to them; how they'd like to be recognized. Involve them in the process that affects them. After you've recognized them in their preferred manner, check back to see if it was truly meaningful. Did they like it? At periodic intervals, ask again . . . and again. Great recognition programs quickly become meaningless recognition programs when we stop asking employees what they want.

Here's what one employee of a local company says, "My manager thanks me ten times a day, for doing things that are really just a part of my job. That means a lot to me and motivates me to work even more conscientiously. He is genuinely grateful for the work I do."

It's not necessarily about money, formal programs, or getting your name in the company newsletter. It's all about what matters to each individual employee.

FAST30

Mentor

O NE OF THE MOST SUCCESSFUL WAYS TO develop your employees is to step up the mentoring program. Mentoring programs can be either formal or informal, and can involve one or more mentors, including yourself. The word *mentor* has its origins in Homer's *Odyssey*. Mentor was Odysseus' wise and trusted counselor, in whose form Athena became the teacher of Odysseus' son, Telemachus. According to *The American Heritage® Dictionary of the English Language, Fourth Edition* the word *mentor* means, "a wise and trusted counselor or teacher" or "to serve as a trusted counselor or teacher, especially in occupational settings."

In a mentoring relationship there is a pairing of the mentor(s) and the mentee or protégé. While it is possible to have an informal mentoring relationship, for best results start out with a formal relationship. Mentors should have the following qualities:

✦ Good listening skills.
✦ Good feedback skills.
✦ Good assessment skills.
✦ Proficiency in the competency area where he or she will be mentoring.
✦ Ability to tap into a variety of resources to help the mentee.

✦ High level of commitment to the mentoring relationship.

Mentees or protégés should have the following qualities:

✦ Result oriented—the desire to set goals and achieve them in a timely way.
✦ Self-direction—the ability to take responsibility for one's own development.
✦ Commitment to use the feedback given by the mentor.
✦ High level of commitment to the mentoring relationship.

Before starting any mentoring relationship, come to an agreement regarding the goals and expectations of the relationship. Put it in writing and refer to it often. Decide on the following:

✦ What skills or competencies does the mentee want to attain?
✦ How can the mentor assist?
✦ How will confidential issues be handled?
✦ How often will you meet?
✦ How long will the relationship last?
✦ How will you assess progress and determine success?

Mentoring relationships can help develop your employees in a way that training programs cannot. The relationship can deal with skill development in a timely way and give immediate feedback, direction, and guidance. Not everyone is cut out to be a mentor, but if you are, this just might help build your staff and enhance the workplace environment.

FAST 31

Understand Coaching Responsibilities

A RE YOU A BOSS OR A COACH? BOSSES DIC-
tate, order, make sure the work gets done, and provide
directions on what to do. Coaches mentor, teach, help
others to become self-directed, and offer direction and
context so people understand what to do. It makes sense
that if you want to build and sustain long-lasting high
performance in your workforce, then the way to do it is
by coaching rather than bossing. Some of the responsibilities of a coach are:

To build the competency levels of staff.

Coaches clearly state what the expected competency level
of staff should be and hold each person accountable for
meeting or exceeding that standard. A good coach can
help an employee pinpoint where he or she is in professional development, define what needs to be done to
reach higher levels, and provide two-way feedback.
Coaches raise the performance standard as needed and
recognize those who exceed the standard. Coaches go to
bat for their people.

To open up possibilities so people can think creatively.

Coaches look to the edges of the organization and are constantly on the lookout for new ways of doing things. A coach challenges each person to do the same and gives "gentle pushes" to achieve goals. Brainstorming, "what if" statements, and other creative thinking techniques are routinely introduced and used. Coaches do not make statements like "We've always done it this way," or "It won't work."

To assist with breakdowns when needed.

Coaches help their people to map the process, locate the breakdown and then clear the path. They help in generating solutions. A coach offers guidance in anticipating the next breakdown and developing ways to avoid it. The coach keeps the focus on the issue, not on any individual's personal shortcomings.

FAST32

Understand How to Coach for CHANGE

COACHES ATTEMPT TO EFFECT SOME TYPE OF behavioral change in an individual or a team. What are the elements needed to set the stage for change? CHANGE is an acronym that stands for the important elements needed for a successful coaching intervention:

+ Contract
+ Handle Difficulties
+ Assess and Approach
+ Negate the Old
+ Give Reinforcement
+ Evaluate and Make Changes

Let's look at these in more detail.

Contract

The first step involves contracting with the individual to build a foundation for the change to occur. This step is key in a successful coaching intervention. A coaching contract is similar to any type of contract: It sets the tone with a clear, workable agreement. When constructing the coaching contract consider the following:

✦ Do all parties share the same understanding of all the terms and conditions of the contract?

✦ Is the intended outcome (goal) stated?

✦ How will attaining or accomplishing this goal be measured?

✦ What are the action steps?

✦ What is the schedule for each step?

✦ Who is accountable for each step along the way?

✦ Who are the players?

✦ What is the feedback mechanism? How does it work?

✦ What follow-up will occur?

Handle Difficulties

It is not unusual for a coach to encounter difficulties, both from the person or people that are being coached and from outside participants. To ensure that the intervention does not become derailed along the way, consider the following:

✦ What difficulties do you anticipate before even starting the intervention? What strategies can you put into place to be proactive in handling these situations?

✦ Do you have a toolbag? If so, do you have all of your tools handy? If not, when will you start building one?

✦ How will you know what resistance looks like? Defensiveness? Anxiety? How will you handle these?

✦ How will you behave if criticized? How will you distinguish if it is a valid criticism of the intervention or an attack on you?

✦ What follow-up mechanism will you put into place? How will you monitor progress?

Assess and Approach

Once you have agreed on the contract and considered how to handle difficulties, it's time to design a coaching approach. It's important to know the person or people you are working with, and then develop appropriate coaching strategies. One size definitely does not fit all!

✦ What is the primary situation that has to be rectified? Is this really the problem? Are there other issues that must be addressed to get to the real problem?

✦ What tools will you use to assess the situation? (Interviews, pencil and paper instruments, data collection methods.)

✦ What is your style? The person or team with whom you are working? What approach is most appropriate given the two styles?

✦ Has anything like this been done in the past? Successes? Failures?

✦ What is your time frame?

✦ Will other people be a part of this?

Negate the Old

Negate means to neutralize, cancel, or counteract. And that's exactly what coaches are trying to do . . . cancel the old, unacceptable behaviors and replace them with new, acceptable behaviors. But, old habits die hard . . . and as human beings we are very much invested in our old ways, even if those old ways yield negative results. In trying to help an employee or team break those old habits, ask yourself these questions:

✦ Does this person realize their patterns? Do you?

✦ What will motivate this person to break the old habits and replace them with new habits?

✦ Is this something that can be done solo or will additional assistance be required?

✦ Can you describe this in quantifiable terms?

✦ How can you discuss this so that emotion does not take over?

✦ What type of follow-up mechanism will be used?

Give Reinforcement

Reinforcement is key in making the new habits stick . . . in getting the type of behavior change you seek. There are many different types of reinforcers. A good coach needs to find the ones that work best. As a note, positive reinforcers are generally more effective in sustaining long-term behavior changes.

Behavior Modification is a program that focuses on managing human activity by controlling the consequences of performing that activity.

✦ Positive reinforcement is a reward that consists of a desirable consequence of behavior.

✦ Negative reinforcement is a reward that consists of the elimination of an undesirable consequence.

✦ Punishment is the presentation of an undesirable behavioral consequence or the removal of a desirable one that decreases the likelihood that the behavior will continue.

Evaluate and Make Changes

As with any course of action, it is important in a coaching intervention to evaluate what is occurring and to make changes to ensure success (as much as possible). The goal, of course, is to have some quantifiable measurement so that you, as a coach, can measure if any change has occurred and to what extent.

+ Is your evaluation or measurement mechanism working?
+ Has the original outcome or goal been achieved?
+ If so, how will you maintain the gain?
+ If not, what are your options? What is the next step?
+ Has the schedule been followed? Have there been changes?
+ Have there been process measurements along the way? What have those measurements shown?
+ Is the employee motivated and committed to improving performance?

FAST 33

Establish Goals and Have
Frequent Goal Meetings

Setting goals is an easy process. Achieving them, however, is not always so easy. One of the easiest ways is to use the tried and true SMART goal formula. Help employees set and reach goals by using the SMART acronym.

   Specific—What needs to be done? What result is desired? Are the goals clearly delineated?

   Measurable—How will you measure success? How will you know the goal has been met?

   Attainable or Action-Oriented—Can the goals be accomplished with reasonable resources? Is it within reach with just a bit of stretching?

   Relevant or Realistic—Is the goal part of what's important in the organization? Can the employee expect to contribute to the bigger picture by successfully completing the goal?

   Timely—When will the goal be complete? Is there a solid commitment to a deadline?

By assisting employees to establish and accomplish important goals, you help to enhance their commitment, motivation, and self-directedness towards the job. It's important to remember, though, that setting goals is not enough. Frequent meetings are important to:

✦ Review progress on goals
✦ Revise goals as organizational priorities dictate
✦ Work through roadblocks
✦ Brainstorm different approaches
✦ Celebrate upon goal completion
✦ Establish new goals

Employees often have conflicting priorities and can spend much of their time on nonessential and nonproductive work. It is your job, as supervisor, to help redirect employees to the "vital few" tasks, rather than spend their time on the "trivial many." This is also called the 80/20 concept or the Pareto Principle (JM Juran, *Managerial Breakthrough*). Some examples of the 80/20 concept are: 80% of absenteeism is caused by 20% of the employees, or 20% of the people do 80% of the talking in any given group. When it comes to working on goals, very often 80% of our employees' effort gets spent on only 20% of the critical work and important goals fall by the wayside. It's very easy to get caught up in the day-to-day crisis, and very soon progress on goals comes to a halt.

That's why it's important to meet on a regular basis with employees and keep them focused on the vital few goals—those goals that will have greatest organizational impact when completed. Very soon, when the sense of accomplishment takes hold, your employees will start to pick up the ball and take responsibility for goal setting and completion.

FAST 34

Know What Your Competition Is Doing

To PARAPHRASE (AND SLIGHTLY CHANGE) A famous quote: "Keep your employees close, but keep your competition closer!" While it's important for you to understand employees and their productivity, it's just as important to have a thorough understanding of those that might influence your employees' decision to leave the company.

Before you can even think about what the competition is doing, know who the competition is. For example, a large non-profit felt that their competition for residential staff was other similar non-profits. Indeed, many former employees seemed to go to these other non-profits on a regular basis; however, when former residential employees were surveyed, it was found that the greatest majority of this group went to completely different industries, such as retail and fast-food. The other non-profits were not the competition; the true competitors for the employee base were Wal-Mart, Burger King and McDonald's.

Having this information allows you to gather better information on what attracts and retains employees in the workplace. Try to be knowledgeable in at least the following areas:

+ What are the demographics of your competitors' workforce?

+ What is the average tenure of employment?

+ What attracts employees to your competition?

+ How does your company's pay and benefits compare with the competition's?

+ What special perks does the competition offer that you don't?

+ What differentiates your competitor's workplace environment from yours?

+ What are the primary and secondary reasons that people leave your company, and how is that satisfied with the new employer?

The answers to these questions will get you started in providing employees with the type of environment that is conducive to long-term employment. Granted, some of these areas require a long-term commitment to change; however, it all starts with asking the right questions and then using the answers to build a strong foundation.

FAST35

Conduct Effective Department and Team Meetings

W HY DO WE HAVE MEETINGS AT ALL? MEET-ings can be useful, and in fact productive if done correctly. Meetings are primarily held because an issue requires the interaction of different people with different perspectives to be solved. Also, group buy-in may be essential.

Do any of the following meeting problems sound familiar?

+ Getting off the subject
+ No goals or agenda
+ Too lengthy
+ Poor or inadequate preparation
+ Inconclusive
+ Disorganized
+ Ineffective leadership or lack of control
+ Irrelevance of information discussed
+ Time wasted during meetings

◆ Starting late

◆ Not effective for decision-making

◆ Interruptions

◆ Dominating individuals

◆ Rambling or digressive discussion

◆ No written results or follow-up action

◆ No pre-meeting orientation/canceled or postponed meetings

— *Source Rochester Institute of Technology, 1992*

There *is* a cure!

Productive meetings that people actually don't mind attending require a bit of work. Before the meeting, do some careful planning. Determine who needs to be there, where and when it will be held, and the general purpose of the meeting. Send out agendas ahead of time so participants can be prepared. And, since you're the chairperson, it's important for you to be there a little early to make sure everything is in order.

Start meetings on time, or as close to the scheduled time as possible. Know how long the meeting will last and end on time. Quickly review the agenda and make any necessary corrections. If needed, assign roles, such as secretary or recorder, timekeeper, or facilitator. Follow the agenda, stay on track, and ensure that all people at the meeting are participating.

Before the meeting ends, establish action items, review achievements, and schedule the next meeting date. If it makes sense, you can even set the agenda or parts of it. Also, you may want to put into place an evaluation mechanism to assess the effectiveness of the meeting.

Have the minutes prepared and distributed to all participants shortly after the meeting. And, prior to the next meeting, gently remind people about action items assigned to them.

When your meetings start and end on time and people attending feel that they've contributed and accomplished something, the negative connotation of "yet another meeting" will start to fade.

FAST36

Understand Different Strategies for Dealing with Conflict

Forming, Storming, Norming, Performing . . . and sometimes Adjourning. These are the stages of team development. Forming, Norming, and Performing usually run fairly smoothly. It's the Storming stage that takes up much of our time and has undermined the efforts of many teams. It's important to understand that every team goes through a Storming stage . . . even the ones that don't admit it. The most successful teams understand that Storming is a normal part of team development, and they effectively deal with the conflict during this stage.

There can be good reason for team conflict, so it's important to move in a positive and proactive way to reduce conflict and get the group back on track. Try some of the following strategies:

✦ Try to deal with the underlying reasons for conflict; use active listening skills.

✦ Be aware of what team members are doing outside of work. If a team member goes to an extreme, there may be problems outside of work that are causing the conflict.

✦ Use subgroups or joint job assignments to help reduce conflict.

✦ Some conflicts, especially between dominant people, may need to be dealt with outside the group.

✦ Focus on the positive side of each person's differences. Each person brings a different strength to the table.

✦ If you want your team to be high-performance, as the Team Leader or Supervisor, you also need to be in a high-performance mode.

✦ If possible, redesign the job to maximize the group's effectiveness.

✦ If you are dealing with multiple conflicts, start with the one that seems easiest to resolve. Go for the quick victory to set a tone of success in conflict resolution.

✦ Do not overlook the possibility that you may be causing or exacerbating the conflict.

✦ People often try to achieve solidarity by attacking a scapegoat, either within or outside the group. This is damaging, and the group should be re-directed.

✦ If necessary, bring in a third person to act as a mediator.

✦ Not all conflict is bad—a moderate amount of conflict is healthy and essential to a well-functioning team.

✦ Do not take any of the hints too far or so literally that they do more harm than good. The techniques and information are guidelines. You need to use judgment when implementing them with your group.

FAST 37

Help Employees Develop a "Big Picture" Focus

AN UNDERLYING PRINCIPLE OF TAE KWON DO states that by understanding the larger perspective, or the big picture, all the details will fall into place. Those skilled in this martial art can handle several attackers at one time. Why? Because the martial artist is reacting to the big picture (all attackers!), rather than worrying about how to throw a punch.

One of the most valuable skills that any individual can bring to an employer is the ability to maintain perspective on the big picture. This is something that every manager can help employees develop. I once had a boss and mentor say to me, "When you're up to your ears in alligators, sometimes it's hard to remember that your mission is to drain the swamp." At that time, I was immersed in a project and fretting over some of the details. He felt that I was spending way too much time on those details and not enough time focusing on my true mission. It's those people who can hold onto the mission, who don't get "mired in the minutiae" that will be perceived as most valuable to the organization.

Here are six important questions to consider when working with employees:

1. Are you helping your organization achieve strategic, operational, and financial advantage by what you do? If you can't answer yes to all three, then think about how your job is structured and what can be done to restructure it.
2. Do you have hard performance measures? Are they based on hard data and are those measures tied to the organization's strategy? Can you easily show the value that you bring to the organization?
3. Do you take a continuous improvement approach to your job or do you rest on laurels from past successes? Do you know when good enough is good enough?
4. Do you keep customers (whether internal or external) at the forefront of your thinking? Do they drive what you do?
5. Do you know how to use technology for competitive advantage? Do you know how to successfully meld "high tech and high touch?"
6. Are you an expert in your part of the organization? Do you share that expertise and are you a resource for others?

The answers to these questions will give you an indication of where your employees' focus is directed. Answering no to any question means that the focus may not be on the bigger picture. When the focus is on the smaller aspects of the organization, the value that each employee brings to the organization decreases. It doesn't matter if that person is a cashier, vice president, or a health care professional. Knowing where each employee fits into the big picture, and how to maximize the contribution within that context, can mean the difference between a big return or a little to no return.

Help employees keep their collective eye on the big picture and watch the details fall into place.

FAST38

Get Rid of the Fickle Finger of Blame

T HE FICKLE FINGER OF BLAME IS AN INSIDIOUS by-product of a work environment steeped in disrespect, low morale, and resistance to trying new and different approaches. The fickle finger of blame inevitably lands on an individual when something has gone wrong and someone has to take the fall or answer to a higher authority (usually your boss). And, you never know when it might land on you.

Accountability and responsibility are admirable attributes to cultivate in all your employees; pointing the fickle finger of blame does not encourage these attributes. In fact, it helps promote the CYA (Cover Your Butt) mentality. Let me give you an example of how this works.

A few years ago, two human resources (HR) professionals were put in charge of a major salary administration overhaul. Part of this overhaul involved rewriting all existing job descriptions. This was no easy task, as there were over 100 job titles. The two HR people tried to involve as many employees and supervisors as possible in the rewrites, and also took into account what executive management wanted. Finally the job description rewrites were completed and distributed. What followed was completely unexpected.

There was an outcry that the job descriptions did not accurately reflect the jobs. So the CEO sat down with the two HR professionals and said it was important for the three of them to apologize to the employees at the next meeting and to assure them that the job descriptions would go back to the drawing board. The CEO felt it was important for them to take responsibility for what had gone wrong.

The two HR people got up at the next meeting and made the public apology. The CEO was conspicuously absent; having successfully pointed the fickle finger of blame in their direction. Needless to say, these two individuals were much more guarded about how they went about their work in the future and approached their work from a, "How can I CYA" mentality.

Had the CEO approached the problem in a more positive, less accusatory, and demoralizing way, the two HR people probably would be more inclined to try new things and take some calculated risks. However, they now approach tasks more cautiously: "How can I cover myself in case we have a problem?"

Here's a positive way to deal with getting rid of the fickle finger of blame. A few years ago, Remedy Corporation wanted to encourage an environment of risk-taking. Although some companies might choose to reward and recognize individuals or teams that were successful in taking risks, Remedy took it one step further. Each employee received one "Take a Chance" card. Managers got more. These were used when an employee took a risk that didn't pan out. No punishment. No negativity. No sweat. Employees are expected to take risks in their jobs, and managers are expected to take even more risks.

Here's an organization that has truly minimized, and perhaps eliminated, the fickle finger of blame. Try these ideas to get you started:

+ Have an expectation that employees will try new things, and if they don't work out, visibly recognize their efforts in trying something new

+ Never criticize or humiliate the person. You're dealing with the work, not the individual.

+ Use the SIMPLE feedback formula (FAST17) to debrief when things run amok.

+ Demonstrate, in some tangible way, that you are getting rid of placing blame. Emphasize that you are all there to work together and act as resources for one another. Some tangible actions might be:

  + Take a Risk or Get Out of Jail Cards.

  + Hold a ceremony that buries the fickle finger of blame.

  + Establish guidelines or ground rules that prevent the fickle finger of blame from landing on anyone.

  + Promote positive reinforcement for efforts.

  + Contract as partners to resolve projects or programs that have gone poorly.

FAST39

Lead the Change in Thinking

"If in the last few years you haven't discarded a major opinion or acquired a new one, check your pulse. You may be dead." (Gelett Burgess, 1866–1951)

P<small>USH YOURSELF TO THE OUTER LIMITS OF YOUR</small> organization. When change is inevitable (and isn't it always?), it is seldom from the core. It is not from those that are heavily invested in the old way of doing things. Changes come from those that have nothing to lose by trying something new.

Think about your own investment in "the way it's always been" thinking. Companies like Intel and Microsoft; people like Alexander Graham Bell and Dr. W. Edwards Demming; advances in health care, like outpatient surgery; or 24-hour sports or news coverage on stations like ESPN or CNN are a result of changes that occurred on the fringes. No one person in the core group was responsible for leading the way. Certainly Microsoft and Intel have given us a completely new philosophy in fast, efficient technology for the masses. Alexander

Graham Bell was not in the mainstream of communications. Dr. W. Edwards Demming had to go to Japan for acceptance of his ideas on total quality. And ESPN and CNN were not born of the mainstream news and sports media of the day.

In a time when work process, technology, and information change at lightning speed, our thought processes are lagging far behind. To set the tone for a change in thinking, try the following exercise:

1. First, identify three or four significant changes that you've witnessed in your organization over the last three to five years. Where did those changes originate? Remember, just because a CEO mandates a new policy or program, it doesn't mean the change originated from that person. Look beyond the confines of the organization to determine the point of origin.

2. Once you've identified the changes and understand where they originated, ask yourself these questions:

   ✦ From what direction are the next changes likely to occur? (Remember, look to the fringes.)

   ✦ Once you've identified the change, what actions will you take?

   ✦ What impact might this change have on your organization or department?

   ✦ What will the impact be if the change occurs and you take no action?

3. Decide, with input from your staff, what to anticipate and what type of action is appropriate to take.

FAST40

Help Your People Adapt to Change

Helping your employees adapt to change requires you to be the Change Agent. The Change Agent is the person who leads the change. The changes that you are orchestrating may be narrow (implementing a new time card system) or broad (altering the culture of an organization). Regardless of the magnitude of the change, Change Agents have common characteristics:

- ✦ Ability to relate to diverse groups of people
- ✦ Ability to determine how a change should be made
- ✦ Problem-solving skills
- ✦ Persuasive influence skills
- ✦ Ability to determine how much change employees can withstand
- ✦ Ability to match internal organizational strengths and weaknesses with external opportunities and threats (See FAST4)
- ✦ Flexibility and responsiveness to change

What happens to organizations when people don't adapt to change? Depending on the stability of the organization, and the time it takes to adapt, there are several possible outcomes.

S **T** **A** **B** **I** **L** **I** **T** **Y**	When stability is high and adaptation time is low, the result is a slow, and sometimes tortuous, death.	When stability is high and adaptation time is high, the result is ability to survive downturns, and subsequent growth.
	When both stability and adaptation time are low, the result is quick death.	When stability is low and adaptation time is high, the result is a false sense of security, followed by a quick death.

ADAPTATION TIME

There are many in-between variations and combinations. This points out the need to not only provide a stable organization, but also to be highly adaptable to change. These guidelines will help you start breaking down the barriers:

✦ Keep the information flowing to your employees. No surprises.

✦ Promote understanding through two-way communication and active listening skills.

✦ Answer questions as honestly as possible.

✦ Walk the talk. Be a Change Agent. Set the tone to positively reinforce whenever possible.

✦ Cascade a positive attitude.

✦ Work incrementally. Make small-scale changes first. Use trial runs.

✦ Go for a quick win to build momentum.

FAST41

Look For Opportunities to Develop Employees' Skills

THERE'S BARELY A DAY THAT GOES BY WHEN WE don't hear about the skills and competencies employees need to develop to take the organization into the future. While intellectually we agree with statements like these, it's more difficult to translate that premise into tangible actions.

One organization has made this a priority. Employees are regularly assessed, in terms of current strengths and developmental needs. These competencies are related to future job opportunities, a position that the employee might aspire to in coming years. Employees find out what competencies they already have that are needed for future job opportunities, and where they must develop additional competencies. Then a plan is put into place to give them the resources to work on their developmental needs.

If you don't have this type of formalized, company-wide program you can establish one, starting with benchmarking from this best practice. Don't wait for a formal program; look for the opportunity to home-grow your employees' skills.

Use the following steps to formulate your own program:

1. Write down the specific skills and competencies needed to take your department to the next level.
2. Assess, in conjunction with the employee, his or her strengths and developmental needs. Use a pencil and paper assessment if possible.
3. Compare, in chart form, the skills you need, what the employee has, and what is needed.
4. Review with the employee and develop a feasible plan, using SMART goals (See FAST32).
5. Review on a regular basis and provide ongoing feedback.

Here's an example of how this can work. In a discussion with an employee, a manager discovered that the employee was bored. This came as a surprise, as the employee was a top producer; there was a high degree of work quality and quantity. The manager started discussing the future of the department. One of the important functions was project monitoring, which involved knowledge in project management, especially budgeting. During the discussion, the manager found out that the employee had a financial analysis background. Together, the manager and employee developed a plan that would allow the employee involvement in project monitoring, without being overwhelmed with current job duties.

It was also discovered that the employee was weak in some specific computer skills that were needed, so the manager arranged for additional one-on-one training. Regular follow-up was scheduled. The end result was an employee that continued to be a solid contributor with the old job, was motivated by the challenges of the new duties, and a manager who didn't have to go to outside resources to satisfy departmental needs. The manager, employee, and company all benefited from this process.

FAST 42

Find the Jewel
(When the Clouds Are Dark)

T HERE'S A TOP-SELLING INSURANCE SALES person that consistently ranks as a super sales person in his company. Each time I see him, we greet each other with, "How's it going?" And each time he says something to the effect of, "Absolutely, fantastically great!"

Sometimes I know that things aren't going great. New business could be off, long-time customers may be switching to another agent, or there might be personal problems that are demanding his attention. But that doesn't seem to matter. One of the secrets to my insurance buddy's success is that he's consistently able to find the jewel.

Keeping focus on the positive—finding the jewel—can determine whether your employees have high or low morale. Most employees expect to deal with a variety of workplace issues, such as lay-offs, salary cuts, unfair policies and practices, and decisions that seem to have no rhyme or reason. Employees also realize that you may not have any control over various situations. The key is to let your employees know that you understand their points of view and then focus on how to deal with the situation in a positive way.

For example, one manager suggests, "Commiserate and take action." If there is a policy or procedure change that doesn't make sense, but must be implemented, this manager tells employees that it doesn't make any sense to her either, but it has to be done, so let's figure out the best way. Some senior leaders may see this as not supporting the company, but this manager of the year argues it's just the opposite. "Employees can see right through bad decisions. Saying that I'm behind it is dishonest and it doesn't build a relationship with employees."

Try these suggestions:

✦ When there is negativity all around, call the group together for a brainstorming session to identify the positives. Then, set quick, attainable goals to reap the rewards of the positive items you've identified.

✦ Brainstorm the negatives. Look at what the group can and can't control. Develop improvement plans for those that are controllable; develop "live with it" plans for those that aren't controllable. The important thing is to not spend any more time or energy on the uncontrollable issues than is absolutely necessary.

✦ Implement a department suggestion program, with meaningful rewards. Non-financial rewards work quite well.

✦ Implement a "fine" system for negativity, similar to the fines many offices had in place a decade or more ago for using foul language.

✦ Provide plenty of positive reinforcement for the gains that have been made.

FAST43

Know When to Raise the Standard Bar

ONE OF THE IMPORTANT RESPONSIBILITIES OF a coach is to develop competencies, and to know when and how to raise the standard bar (FAST31). What are the signs that it's time to raise the standard bar?

✦ Employees' work is routinely completed with a high level of quality, long before deadline.

✦ Employees seem to be exhibiting symptoms of boredom with their current work assignments.

✦ Creativity seems to be stifled or non-existent.

✦ Employees regularly (or even irregularly) ask for new tasks.

✦ Employees request professional development in areas that are more relevant to future assignments.

✦ The department or individual employees seem to be on "auto-pilot."

Raising the standard bar requires a great deal of judgment and finesse. Certainly you want employees to stretch to higher levels of achievement. However, you don't want them to stretch so much that it is counterproductive. To gently raise the standard bar, try these techniques:

✦ Raise the bar incrementally. Decide where the new standard should be and then identify three to five steps that will lead to the new standard. Work with the employee to reach the incremental steps.

✦ Set a deadline. There is great power in knowing that something must be done by a specific date. Develop a plan with the employee that allows them to reach the new standard by the stated deadline.

✦ Help the employee to raise his or her own standard bar. Coach them to self-identify the new standard. Work with them to decide when the standard should be kicked up a notch, without prompting from you.

✦ Use if-then statements. For example, "If we are to cut expenses by 20%, then we will have to _____." Both you and the employee can mutually decide how to fill in the blank.

FAST 44

Use Failure as a Vehicle For Success

WE ALL EXPERIENCE FAILURE DURING OUR careers. In fact, it's said that success can only be born out of experiencing failure. Do the following statements sound familiar?

+ Failed in business in 1831
+ Defeated for Legislature in 1832
+ Second failure in business in 1833
+ Suffered nervous breakdown in 1836
+ Defeated for Speaker in 1838
+ Defeated for Elector in 1840
+ Defeated for Congress in 1843
+ Defeated for Congress in 1848
+ Defeated for Senate in 1855
+ Defeated for Vice President in 1856
+ Defeated for Senate in 1858
+ Elected President in 1860

The person who experienced these eleven failures was one of our greatest presidents, Abraham Lincoln. What if he had given up after his first failure, or even the second or third? Success does not come easily. What's important about our failures is that we learn from them.

It's especially critical to focus employees on what can be done to improve the next time. Morale can plummet and employees may be hesitant to expose themselves to another failure. Managers can help employees work through failure by taking a positive stance.

Some suggestions:

+ Debrief the employee after an unsuccessful project, meeting, or whatever was involved. Dissect each step of the project, looking at the actions that were taken at each step. Determine where the project went off track and what can be done in the future to prevent derailment.

+ Look at the positive aspects of the project. Find something that is worthy of praise. Then ask the employee what he or she would change if it could be done over.

+ Use a force field analysis to look at the forces that helped the project be successful and those that hindered project success. Analyze each, paying particular attention to those that were within the employee's control.

+ Offer to assist the employee in mapping out the critical path of the next project. Identify checkpoints where you'll be available to discuss the project to ensure the work is on track.

+ Offer reassurance and encouragement. Even one of our most beloved presidents had his share of personal and work-related failures. Success comes on the heels of failure. Encourage your employees to squarely face those failures and use them as learning points to reach higher levels of success.

FAST 45

Understand the Dynamics in the Organization

I T'S TRUE. THE NEW PROGRAMS, CHANGES, AND improvements won't amount to much if they're squelched from above. Although your technical competency has, at least partially, gotten you to a management position, it's often understanding the intricacies of "how things work" at your organization that will make you a continued success. Sometimes you just need to learn different dances, how to build alliances, and stay under the radar.

Learning the dynamics of your organization can help you understand when and where to make your case. Here's what happened to one manager.

The weekly management meeting was often a quagmire of accusations and innuendo, and in fact, you never knew where the fickle finger of blame would point at any given moment. After one particularly brutal meeting (where a senior manager was ridiculed and severely chastised), our manager was overcome with a sense of rightness. She went to the CEO and said that she didn't want to be a part of a meeting that humiliated people. She explained that it just wasn't right and definitely not consistent with the culture that the organization was striving to create. The CEO listened to her thoughtfully and asked her if there was anything else she wanted to add. The manager said, "No," though she hoped the CEO understood where she was coming from. He replied that indeed he did, and he told her that she would not have to witness such behavior again. She thanked the CEO for his time and went back to her office, feeling as if a burden had been lifted from her highly ethical shoulders.

And lifted it was! That was the last meeting she went to for quite some time. It went something like this, "Since your boss is here, it's really not necessary to have both of you." This manager was learning to dance, but she stepped on too many seasoned toes, too early in the dance. Following the lead of the CEO, no one wanted to be her dance partner.

Although her position was one that was based in rightness and high ethical standards, she didn't understand the dynamics of the organization. Because of her ignorance, relationships with other departments were compromised and her own department staff suffered from the backlash.

A word on radar and alliances. Flying under the radar simply means getting the job done while massaging policy and procedure, but not enough to be scrutinized by upper management. I am not advocating deliberately going against policy and procedure. I am advocating having a thorough understanding so that you know how to massage the system. The alliances are the infrastructure built among employees at the company. It's an informal, underground system that keeps things moving and gets the job done. Even though not on any organization chart, it's just as important.

To truly be in a position to effect changes in your department, solidify workplace alliances, learn different dances and know how to fly under the radar.

FAST46

Give Employees Authority to Solve Problems

An old piece of advice that is regularly given to employees is, "Be a problem solver! Don't ever go to your boss with the problem . . . let him or her know how you have solved it or intend to solve it!" Sound advice . . . I think. Wouldn't it be great if employees effectively solved all their own problems, and only came to you to let you know the solution and outcome? Fantasy, you say? Only in organizations that don't give authority to employees to solve the everyday problems that inevitably crop up.

The first step is to teach employees the basic problem-solving steps.

1. Define the problem exactly as it exists (no adjectives . . . they elicit unneeded emotion). Problem statements should not imply a solution. For example, "The monthly management staffing reports have been two weeks late for the past three months because the computer system keeps going down." This immediately closes you off to potential solutions because it implies the computer system is at

fault. This could be a potential cause, but without adequate data collection and information sharing, you can't be certain. You may also end up of fixing a superfluous contributing cause, not the root cause of the problem. Writing a good problem statement is the most important step in the process.

2. Define what you see as the ideal state (what "it" will look like when the problem's solved). This will give you focus on where you're going and help in planning how you'll get there.

3. Write down the consequences, both positive and negative, that the problem has on your organization. This will help focus and add validity as to whether or not this is a problem, and also give credence to the magnitude of the problem.

4. Determine possible root causes. Validate and reanalyze, using appropriate tools. Validate with data. This might mean postponing a decision until data can be gathered.

5. What is your original problem statement? Is it still relevant considering the data that has been gathered?

6. Generate possible solutions. Use brainstorming techniques. Remember, nothing is too crazy or outside the box!

7. Select a possible solution. Ensure that there has been an objective analysis of the data.

8. Check to see if resources are available to implement the solution.

9. Determine how you will evaluate—how will you know that the solution has worked?

Educating your employees and mentoring them to become good problem solvers will help you be more effective in your job. If you want employees to become problem solvers, give them the tools to do it right.

FAST47

Heat Up the Iron and Then Strike While It's Hot

Timing is everything . . . well, almost. Astute supervisors can sense when the timing is right for certain events, and then use this knowledge to their competitive advantage. Competitive advantage also includes improving the workplace environment. Strike while the iron's hot.

However, if the iron never gets hot, it can be difficult to do. Here's a few ways to build momentum:

1. Start small. Often it's hardest just to get started. If you can choose to start with issues or areas of lesser concern, it will be easier to achieve success. Save the big stuff for when you have a few successes under your belt. For example, you may want your employees to become more self-motivated (is there any other kind?). That is a worthy goal, but also a big one—difficult to achieve and often the by-product of other environmental and management issues.

   Maybe an employee has mentioned that a form should be redesigned or has an idea for better department coverage. Compared to motivation, these are fairly simple projects. They are very task oriented. When someone is involved in a project that has clearly defined tasks, it's much easier to clearly see the successful outcome.

2. Make sure there is clear and public recognition, on both an individual, departmental and organizational basis.

3. Once you have a few successes under your belt (like the redesigned form or the department coverage), it's time to move to bigger and better things. It's time to strike while the iron's hot! Your employees will know how success feels, and since you've paid attention and been a part of the growth curve, they'll probably be more willing to undertake the bigger projects and issues.

This is by no means a guarantee that all will go as planned. There will be hurdles along the way. But, that's part of your job . . . to remove the roadblocks that keep your employees from achieving higher levels of productivity and job satisfaction. Remember, this is a learning process and you must give employees the opportunity to do just that. . . learn.

FAST48

Know Your Employees' Other Sides

Like Darth Vader and his son, Luke Sky-walker, everyone has two sides. Ours may not come down to good and evil, but certainly we have a work side and a personal side. Too often, supervisors only get to know the work side of a person. Not only doesn't this give a well-rounded view of their employees, but it also cuts them away from information that might be critical in developing employees to their fullest potential.

We're told by misguided management gurus not to mix business with our employees' personal lives, but in following that advice we miss the boat on what may well be the most important information of all.

I'm not advocating cocktails every night after work—something a little more subtle works just as well. Try these conversation starters to help to get to know your staff better.

1. How was your (weekend, vacation, bowling league, softball game . . . you get the picture)?
2. What do you do when you're not here slaving away?

3. What are your kids involved in?
4. I saw your (fill in the blank—daughter, son, spouse, cousin, etc.) in the paper. What he or she is doing sounds great! Tell me more about it.
5. Let's grab a bite to eat—what's your favorite eating place?
6. Those are great or that's a great (fill in the blank— shoes, slacks, pen, wall hanging, picture, vase, etc.). Where did you get it?

These comments and questions aren't going to save the world. They may even seem simplistic, which begs the question, "Why don't we engage in these types of conversations more often?" Taking the first step to engage an employee in a non-work related conversation opens up new possibilities. And by finding out what those new possibilities are, you may uncover a key to building an exceptional work environment.

FAST49

Be Creative to Bring in the Best and Brightest

M ANY YEARS AGO, I WAS IN CHARGE OF recruiting manager trainees for a retail drugstore chain. It seemed that no matter how many advertisements we placed in the paper, how many job fairs we attended, or how many employee referrals we received, we always needed more trainees. We knew that we needed to step outside the box and come up with some creative approaches for recruiting or our competition would snap up all the "good ones." We needed a way to attract the best and brightest.

Competition? That got us thinking. Why only think about competition in negative terms? Instead of fearing the competition, why not figure out a way to use what they do well to our own competitive advantage? The seeds were planted!

It was evident that the larger variety stores had fairly extensive Health and Beauty Aids (HBA) sections. Surely, an HBA manager might want to move up into his or her own store, rather than continuing to work under a large store manager. I began to walk through the HBA sections. If the department looked good, I'd ask for the HBA manager and compliment him or her on how nice the section looked. (I was specific . . . the shelves are well-stocked or the floors looked great—someone really knew how to run a buffer!) This may not seem like a big thing, but in actuality, it was the deal maker! You see, the only time someone commented on the HBA section was when the district manager was yelling at the HBA manager. The compliments went a long way. I'd also discreetly hand my card over and say, "If you know anyone looking for a manager trainee position, with the intention of moving into their own store within a year, please tell them to give me a call." Needless to say, the phone would ring!

What did I know about my competition? I knew that they had a reputation for hiring top-notch people. My competitor was large enough to offer pay and benefits that I could not offer up front. However, I also knew that my competition had a slow-moving career path and that advancement meant moving far away. Store managers had a typical tenure of 10 to 15 years . . . far too long for a high potential department manager to wait. Most of these department managers had a local family and did not want to move. Our organization was able to use all of these factors to our competitive advantage, and in the long run attracted the best and brightest manager trainees.

Understand Your Own Weaknesses

SOMETIMES WE'RE HESITANT TO USE "HARD" WORDS. The word *weakness* has been replaced by *developmental need*. However, it's our own weakness that blinds us to what truly needs to be done to build an exceptional workplace environment.

In *The Five Temptations of a CEO*, author Patrick Lencioni tells in a narrative fashion, why CEOs fail. Although this is written with the CEO in mind, its learning points can be used by anyone in a management position. The five temptations come down to poor choices. In short, they are:

1. Choosing status over results.
2. Choosing popularity over accountability.
3. Choosing certainty over clarity.
4. Choosing harmony over productive conflict.
5. Choosing invulnerability over trust.

As managers, we make these choices, and when the former is chosen over the latter, our employees suffer. When faced with these hard choices, it's important to think in the long-term. Poor choices come from a short-term, self-promoting focus. To avoid yielding to the temptations, it's important to have upward communication. Managers need to have a conduit for information that employees can offer, anonymously if needed. It's also important to be willing to take a hard look at how these temptations affect us.

Avoiding these five downfalls requires forethought and a mindset of continuous improvement. Ask yourself these questions:

1. Do I put more emphasis on my position in the organization than the long-term well being of the organization as a whole?
2. Am I willing to ask my employees tough questions and hold them accountable for the answers?
3. Do I put off decision making because I'm afraid of being wrong or do I focus on clarifying information so that I can make decisions quickly and confidently?
4. Do I seek out diverse opinions from my department or team, and facilitate discussion where all opinions are valued?
5. Are you willing to admit (to others) when you're wrong or do you enter a "spin zone" that justifies your position?

The answers to these questions will give you some clarity on whether or not you're yielding to the temptations. Better yet, let your employees anonymously respond to these questions. The answers you get may be surprising. But, the true surprise comes when you make changes and see a noticeable workplace improvement.

FAST51

Treat Your Employees Like Customers

CUSTOMERS FREQUENTLY GET OUR BEST, AND whatever is left over goes to our employees. Employees are really our customers, too. They are our internal customers, and as important to our core business as the external, or paying, customers.

If we applied the principals of customer loyalty to employee loyalty, we just might see a decrease in turnover and an increase in motivation and loyalty. There are four significant factors (the Factorial Four) of building and maintaining loyalty.

1. The Build, Cement, or Destroy Factor

Every interaction you have with employees (your internal customers), has the potential to either build, cement, or destroy the relationship. Customers want relationships based in authenticity and trust. When customers don't understand us, we've violated that trust. When we don't deal with them authentically, we violate that trust.

It is all about communication. I don't just mean verbal communication. There are many methods to communicate, including e-mail, fax, and tele-conference. Choose your words and presentation formats to make your employees most comfortable. Our buzzwords may not be theirs, especially for newer employees, and may even make them uncomfortable or put them in an underdog position. Efforts to dazzle can blind.

2. The Potentially Most Important Resource: People

In this day of massive meltdowns and layoffs, mergers and acquisitions, the emphasis on people is all the more critical. Why are people so important? Because the personal relationship is still at the core of the customer relationship. Employees want to work with people that they believe are genuinely interested in them, who speak their language, and seem to have a vested interest in their success.

Don't be afraid to put your money . . . your budget . . . where your mouth is. Resources for development are critical to a healthy organization. Try to keep the flames alive once the spark has been lit. It's a lot like romance: dating, marriage, honeymoon, and then the day to day. Keep that romantic spark! After all, if you're not romancing your employees day in, day out, year in, year out, someone else will!

3. Touchy or Techie

The most successful companies will effectively meld high tech with high touch. Technology doesn't necessarily give us more free time, does it? Use it carefully and understand your metrics. Use metrics to lend clarity and track employee behavior, and to improve employee loyalty and retention. How can you use this to better understand your employees as human beings . . . rather than objects or commodities?

Even with the advantages that technology brings, employees still need a face-to-face or voice-to-voice relationship. Employees want to be able to take advantage of all the bells and whistles that high tech brings, but they also need a human hand to walk them through it.

4. The Button It Up and Sew It On Phenomenon

Our family routinely uses Dewitt Cleaners. They are not the cheapest and definitely not the closest dry cleaners to our home. What makes Dewitt Cleaners stand out is the fact that I notice the differences and truly appreciate them. What are the differences? It's the buttons and seams. If a shirt is missing a button, they sew it on. If a pair of pants has a ripped seam, they sew it up. They do this without being asked. They usually let us know when the cleaning is picked up that it's been done, at no charge. This is what makes a difference; this is what is appreciated.

Ask your employees what is it that you do that makes a difference to them . . . what do they truly appreciate, and then use that to build loyalty.

Here's the question: In your last experience or interaction with me, what was most memorable? That's right . . . memorable. The answer to that question, or lack thereof, will help you help your internal customers recognize and appreciate your differences and build loyalty.

FAST52

Know How to Sustain Improvements

Y OU'RE SITTING IN A STAFF MEETING. SOMEONE brings up the topic of improving organizational communications. Everyone is in agreement that communication is definitely something that needs improvement. As all heads are nodding in the affirmative, someone says, "Yeah . . . but we did a training on communication last year, and it didn't help!"

Think about how many new processes you've implemented that have fallen by the wayside or training that's been attended that was forgotten a week later. What happened? Perhaps, it wasn't relevant or useful. Most likely there was no mechanism in place to sustain a long-term change. Use the SUSTAIN acronym:

Systematic
Understanding
Small Piece Plans
Tolerance
Accountability
Investment Mentality
Navigate

Systematic

To ensure --the changes you've put into place stick, it's important to have a systematic plan in place. The plan should outline what needs to happen, who needs to do it, time lines, and expected results. Review the plan regularly (once a week or so) with the relevant players, and tweak as necessary. You also need a systematic way to communicate, make changes, provide resources, and address issues and conflicts as they arise. Leaving these items to chance is risking failure.

The most direct path between two points may be a straight line, but it's highly unlikely that will be the path you take. Anticipate potholes, roadblocks, and other detours. Road hazards come from all directions: employees, managers, the organization, customers, and you. Learn to be flexible and to entertain more than one way of going from Point A to Point B. Be prepared to use contingency plans, because we all know that "the best laid plans . . . ."

Understanding

Your understanding:

+ Do you understand the situation as it exists? The desired state?

+ Do you have an understanding of the resources that will be needed?

+ Do you have an understanding of your employees' skill sets and what they will need to implement and sustain the change?

+ Do you understand the employees' perceptions of their work environment and the impact of this change?

Employees' understanding:

◆ Do employees fully understand the situation?
◆ Has there been any level of involvement up to the present?
◆ What communication systems are in place to promote employee understanding?

Organizational understanding:

◆ Do the "powers-that-be" understand how this change will impact and improve your department or team?
◆ Is there support, both in words and resources, for you?

Small Piece Plans

The rest of the business world does not stop while you're trying to build and sustain an exceptional workplace environment. There may be other projects and work assignments that take your time. There may be constant fires to put out. There are many reasons why time constraints prevent us from carrying out this program.

Your intentions are good . . . but sometimes . . .

That's why it's important to develop a plan that can be implemented on a piece-by-piece basis. It's very similar to the old adage about eating an elephant . . . one bite at a time!

If you're fortunate enough to be able to implement everything at once, great! But for most of us, it's on a piece-by-piece basis. Use realistic scheduling tools and significant checkpoints.

Tolerance

Tolerance is not only for the people with whom you're working, but also for yourself. You will stumble. Your people will stumble. You may try new techniques and not get the expected results. Your people will become frustrated because "it takes too long." You, too, may become frustrated.

This is an evolutionary process. We are all human and, as with any change, it takes time and practice to fully integrate a new way of doing something. Cut yourself and the people that report to you some slack. A word of caution, however. Don't cut so much slack that you lower the standard bar or deviate from the path that will help you attain your goals.

Accountability

The buck stops with you. You are in charge. The success or lack of success is solely upon you. You are the manager or supervisor, and therefore have the power to ensure that changes are made where they are most needed. If you don't have that power, think twice about implementing something new. Power, authority, and accountability. All incredibly energizing when properly channeled.

Do you have employees that don't want to get with the program? It's up to you to get them there. What standards you set and expect people to accomplish are almost totally dependent on you. Nothing will change if you aren't leading the change. Don't have the time? Then don't expect anyone else to have time, either. The fact is, you don't have the time not to develop and coach your people, and demand accountability. You can always go back to the good old days . . . and spend those days playing catch-up.

Investment Mentality

Merriam-Webster's Collegiate Online Dictionary defines *investment* as "the outlay of money usually for income or profit: capital outlay." The word *investment* implies a risk factor. As a manager, the outlay of money comes in the form of hiring and turnover costs. The profit, of course, is a high-performing employee, which takes time. Anyone who went through the roller coaster ride of the 2001 stock market knows that short-term investing can be disastrous. It's a long-term, strategic view that nets the highest profits. When investing in employees, look at the long-term goals and be willing to effectively deal with the highs and lows that often accompany a learning curve.

Navigate

Prepare for the next level. Always anticipate where you and your employees need to be, and be prepared to move there at a moment's notice. Build momentum and be able to strike while the iron's hot (FAST47). Know how to effectively navigate within your organization so that you can lead your employees to achieving their goals. Teach your employees to navigate themselves by clearly communicating goals and mentoring them during the process.

52 Resources
for a Better Workplace

The following is by no means a comprehensive listing of resource reading; however, it's a good start, and you may just find one or two books to help you on your FAST52 journey.

Ahlrichs, Nancy S. *Competing for Talent: Key Recruitment and Retention Strategies for Becoming an Employer of Choice.* Palo Alto, CA: Davies-Black Publishing, 2001.

Barbazette, Jean. *Successful New-Employee Orientation: Assess, Plan and Evaluate Your Program with CD-ROM.* San Francisco, CA: Jossey-Bass Inc., Publishers, 2001.

Barner, Robert W. *Team Troubleshooter: How to Find and Fix Team Problems.* Palo Alto, CA: Davies-Black Publishing, 2001.

Blanchard, Kenneth et al. *High Five: The Magic of Working Together.* New York, NY: Morrow, Williams & Co., 2000.

Branham, F. Leigh. *Keeping the People Who Keep You in Business: 24 Ways to Hang on to Your Most Valuable Talent.* New York, NY: AMACOM, 2000.

Bruce, Anne and James S. Pepitone. *Motivating Employees.* New York, NY: McGraw-Hill Professional, 1998.

Buckingham, Marcus and Curt Coffman. *First, Break All the Rules: What the World's Greatest Managers Do Differently.* New York, NY: Simon and Schuster Trade, 1999.

Catlette, Bill and Richard Hadden. *Contented Cows Give Better Milk.* Germantown, TN: Williford Communications, 2000.

Charan, Ram, Drotter, Steve and Jim Noel. *The Leadership Pipeline: How to Build the Leadership Powered Company.* San Francisco, C.: Jossey-Bass Inc., Publishers, 2000.

Cohen, David S. *The Talent Edge: A Behavioral Approach to Hiring, Developing and Keeping Top Performers.* New York, NY: Wiley, Johns & Sons, Inc., 2001.

Cohen, Dr. Norman H. *A Step By Step Guide to Starting an Effective Mentoring Program.* Amherst, MA: Human Resource Development Press, 2000.

Collins, James. *Good to Great: Why Some Companies Make the Leap . . . And Others Don't.* New York, NY: HarperCollins Publishers, 2001.

Covey, Stephen R. *The 7 Habits of Highly Effective People.* New York, NY: Simon & Schuster Trade, 1989.

Crandall, Rick. *Break-Out Creativity: Bringing Creativity to the Workplace.* Corte Madera, CA: Select Press, 1997.

Crane, Thomas, Parker, Lerissa Nancy, and Troy S. Parker. (Illustrator). *The Heart of Coaching: Using Transformational Coaching to Create a High Performance Culture* - Rev. Ed. Ronkonoma, NY: FTA Press, 2001.

Daniels, Aubrey C. *Bringing Out the Best In People.* New York, NY: McGraw-Hill Professional, 1999.

Deblieux, Mike. *Supervisor's Guide to Employee Performance Reviews.* LEXIS Publishing, 1999.

Elton, Chester and Adrian Robert Gostick. *Managing With Carrots: Using Recognition to Attract and Retain the Best People.* Salt Lake City, UT: Gibbs Smith, 2001.

Godin, Seth. *Survival Is Not Enough: Zooming, Evolution and the Future of Your Company.* New York, NY: The Free Press, 2001.

Gust, Suzanne. *Not So Basic New Hire Orientation.* Spring Lake, MI: Training & Consulting, Inc., 2000.

Hacker, Carol A. *How to Compete in the War for Talent: A Guide to Hiring the Best.* Sanford, FL: Douglas Charles, Limited, 2001.

Herman, Roger E. *Keeping Good People: Strategies for Solving the #1 Problem Facing Business Today.* Winchester, VA: OakHill Press, 1998.

Huszczo, Gregory E. *Tools for Team Excellence: Getting Your Team Into High Gear and Keeping It There.* Palo Alto, CA: Davies-Black Publishing, 1996.

Johnson, Spencer and Kenneth Blanchard. *Who Moved My Cheese? An Amazing Way to Deal with Change in Your Work and in Your Life.* New York, NY: The Putnam Publishing Group, 1998.

Katzenbach, Jon R. and Doug K. Smith. *The Discipline of Teams: A Mindbook-Workbook for Delivering Small Group Performance.* New York, NY: Wiley, Johns & Sons, Inc., 2001.

Klinvex, Kevin, O'Connell, Matthew and Christopher Klinvex. *Hiring Great People.* New York, NY: McGraw-Hill Professional, 1998.

Langdon, Ken and Christine Osborne. *Essential Managers: Performance Reviews.* New York, NY: Dorling Kindersley Publishing, Incorporated, 2001.

Lencioni, Patrick. *The Five Temptations of a CEO: A Leadership Fable.* San Francisco, CA: Jossey-Bass Inc., Publishers, 1998.

Leonard, Dorothy and Walter Swap. *When Sparks Fly: Igniting Creativity in Groups.* Boston, MA: Harvard Business School, 1999.

MacMillan, Pat. *The Performance Factor: Unlocking the Secrets of Teamwork.* Nashville, TN: Broadman & Holman Publishers, 2001.

Maguire, Francis X. and Steve Williford. *You're the Greatest: How Validated Employees Can Impact Your Bottom Line.* Germantown, TN: Williford Communications, 2001.

Maxwell, John C. *The 21 Irrefutable Laws of Leadership: Follow Them and People Will Follow You.* Nashville, TN: Thomas Nelson, 1998.

Maxwell, John C. *The 17 Indisputable Laws of Teamwork: Embrace Them and Empower Your Team.* Nashville, TN: Thomas Nelson, 2001.

Michaels, Ed, Handfield-Jones, Helen and Beth Axelrod. *The War for Talent.* Boston, MA: Harvard Business School, 2001.

Murray, Margo. *Beyond the Myths and Magic of Mentoring: How to Facilitate an Effective Mentoring Process*, Revised Edition. San Francisco, CA: Jossey-Bass Inc., Publishers, 2001.

Napier, Rod, Sanaghan, Patrick, Sidle, Clint and Patrick Saraghan. *High Impact Tools and Activities for Strategic Planning: Creative Techniques for Facilitating Your Organization's Planning Process.* New York, NY: McGraw-Hill Professional, 1997.

Nash, Sue. *Turning Team Performance Inside Out: Team Types and Temperament for High Impact Results.* Palo Alto, CA: Davies-Black Publishing, 1999.

Neal, James E. *Effective Phrases for Performance Appraisals: A Guide to Successful Evaluations,* Ninth Edition. Perrysburg, OH: Neal Publications, Inc., 2000.

Regan, Michael D. *The Journey to Teams: The New Approach to Achieve Breakthrough Business Performance.* Chelan, WA: Holden Press, 1999.

Rinke, Wolf J. *Winning Management: 6 Fail-Safe Strategies for Building High Performance Organizations.* Clarksville, MD: Achievement Publishers, 1997.

Russo, Anthony T. *Minimizing Employee Turnover by Focusing on the New Hire Process.* Upublish.com, 2000.

Schmidt, Warren H., Hateley, BJ Gallagher and Sam Weiss. *Is It Always Right to Be Right?: A Tale of Transforming Workplace Conflict into Creativity and Collaboration.* New York, NY: AMACOM, 2001.

Searles, George J. *Workplace Communications: The Basics.* Boston, MA: Allyn & Bacon, Inc., 1999.

Senge, Peter M. *The Fifth Discipline: The Art and Practice of the Learning Organization.* Garden City, NJ: Doubleday & Company Incorporated, 1990.

Sims, Doris M. *Creative New Employee Orientation Programs: Best Practices, Creative Ideas, and Activities for Energizing Your Orientation Program.* New York, NY: McGraw-Hill Professional, 2001.

Smart, Bradford D. *Topgrading: How Leading Companies Win By Hiring, Coaching and Keeping the Best People.* Paramus, NJ: Prentice Hall Press, 1999.

Still, Del J. *High Impact Hiring: How to Interview and Select Outstanding Employees.* Dana Point, CA: Management Development Systems, 1997.

Thomas, Kenneth W. *Intrinsic Motivation at Work: Building Energy and Commitment.* San Francisco, CA: Berrett-Koehler Publishers, 2000.

Tulgan, Bruce. *Winning the Talent Wars: How to Build a Lean, Flexible, High-Performance Workplace.* New York, NY: W. & Company, Inc., 2002.

Whitworth, Laura, House, Henry, Sadahl, Phil and Henry House-Kimsey. *Go-Active Coaching: New Skills for Coaching People Toward Success in Work and Life.* Palo Alto, CA: Davies-Black Publishing, 1998.

Yate, Martin. *Hiring the Best: A Manger's Guide to Effective Interviewing,* 4th Edition. Holbrook, MA: Adams Media, 1997.

Zemke, Ron and Kristin Anderson. *Coaching Knock Your Socks Off Service.* New York, NY: AMACOM, 1996.

Ordering Information

Order *FAST52 - Building An Exceptional Workplace Environment*

Use this form or fax the entire sheet to:

Ardan Press
PO Box 4234
Rome, NY 13442
Fax: (315) 339-6797

Order direct by calling The Ford Group toll free at 1-888-722-9876

Please send _____ copies @ $14.95 each   _____

Shipping and handling at $3.00/book   _____

Total   _____

Volume discounts available - call the toll free number above for information. Shipping discounts available for orders of four books or more.

Payment by: ☐ Check/Money Order (Payable to "Ardan Press")

☐ Visa ☐ MasterCard Signature: _____

CC#: _____ Exp. Date: _____

Name: _____

Organization: _____

Address: _____

City/State/Zip: _____

We also provide books custom designed with your company's logo, an introduction by your CEO or an introduction written specifically for your company. Call for details!

For information on bringing Lynda Ford to your organization as a conference or meeting speaker, call 1-888-722-9876 or visit the web-site at www.fordgroup.com.